COLLECTOR'S GUIDE TO TV Memorabilia
1960s & 1970s

Greg Davis and Bill Morgan

COLLECTOR BOOKS
A Division of Schroeder Publishing Co., Inc.

The current values in this book should be used only as a guide. They are not intended to set prices, which vary from one section of the country to another. Auction prices, as well as dealer prices, vary greatly and are affected by condition as well as demand. Neither the Authors nor the Publisher assumes responsibility for any losses that might be incurred as a result of consulting this guide.

Searching For A Publisher?

We are always looking for knowledgeable people considered to be experts within their fields. If you feel that there is a real need for a book on your collectible subject and have a large, comprehensive collection, contact Collector Books.

On the Cover: (Clockwise): The Bionic Woman bubble gum card box, $15.00 – $20.00; The Brady Bunch board game, $100.00 – $125.00; Charlies' Angels colorforms, $30.00 – $40.00; Family Affair Mrs. Beasley rag doll, $30.00 – $40.00; Wonder Woman jigsaw puzzle, $10.00 – $15.00; Bewitched coloring book, $25.00 – $35.00; The Partridge Family lunch box, $50.00 – $75.00; I Dream of Jeannie comic book #2, $30.00 – $40.00; Farrah jigsaw puzzle, $15.00 – $20.00.

Cover design: Beth Summers
Book design: Beth Ray

Additional copies of this book may be ordered from:

COLLECTOR BOOKS
P.O. Box 3009
Paducah, Kentucky 42002-3009

@$24.95. Add $2.00 for postage and handling.

Copyright: Greg Davis and Bill Morgan, 1996

CONTENTS

ACKNOWLEDGMENTS

There are several people we wish to thank for contributing to this book in various ways. Not only do we wish to thank them, but we'd expect bodily harm if we didn't.

First we'd like to give special thanks to Nancy Stursa for helping make this book possible. This memorabilia collection all began when she gave Greg a pack of Three's Company trading cards. That one pack grew into a collection of over 5,000 pieces and still continues to grow. Thank you for starting what has been the most enjoyable hobby either of us has ever had.

We'd also like to thank Steve Van Antwerp, our collecting comrade and proof-reader, with whom we've learned the art of collecting. We've made several mis-takes along the way, including cutting up a box of Charlie's Angels trading cards and throwing away all of the wrappers. Who needed all the wrappers? We just wanted to keep one with our sets. Together we've learned the value of saving everything. What may seem worthless today may become valuable in the future.

Special thanks to Charles Chamberlain for his efforts in helping make this book possible, and Casey Chamberlain for adding life to the Halloween costumes.

Finally, we would like to thank our friends and co-collectors who graciously allowed us to photograph the following items from their collections:

Lisa Sutton — The Beverly Hillbillies frame tray puzzles and lunch box; The Bionic Woman lunch box (opening car door on back); The Brady Bunch cigar bands, puzzle, and fun sets; Donny & Marie diary and lunch boxes; Family Affair lunch box; Flipper record and lunch box; The Flying Nun 4" doll and lunch box; H. R. Pufnstuf lunch box; Happy Days Fonzie doll, Richie doll, and lunch boxes; The Hardy Boys T-shirt, guitar, and lunch box; Kung Fu lunch box; The Krofft Supershow lunch box; Lenny & Squiggy dolls; The Love Boat figures; Land of the Lost lunch box; The Mod Squad comic book #5; Mork and Mindy metal lunch box; The New Zoo Revue bendie, Kontrell board game, erasers, lunch box, mobile, and Rushton Freddy; The Partridge Family bus, booklet, clock face, David Cassidy comic books, Laurie and Patti dolls, 1971 fan club kit, guitar, giant puzzle, blue and yellow paper doll boxes, blue paper doll booklet (with 2nd Chris), pin-on button tree, radio, Ricky Segall 45, Crossword Puzzle LP, Laurie House LP, Young Mr. Cassidy paper-back book, and Shopping Bag song book; Sigmund and the Sea Monsters lunch box; Welcome Back Kotter lunch box, classroom, and Barbarino brunch bag.

Bryan Thomas — The Bionic Woman doll (without mission purse); Charlie's Angels paint by numbers set, toy watch, luggage set, sunglasses, wallet, small Corgi van, and poster art kit by Board King; Farrah pillow, grow-hair styling center, dressing room, mugs, cups, and tumblers; Kristy McNichol doll; The Six Mil-lion Dollar Man doll; Wonder Woman dolls.

Giselle Knight — Bewitched Samantha doll; CHiPs Ponch and Jon dolls; Marie Osmond 30" doll; Family Affair 1969 Buffy paper doll booklet; Happy Days Ralph and Potsie dolls; Welcome Back Kotter dolls and jigsaw puzzle #450-03.

Nancy Stursa — The Beverly Hillbillies 1964 yellow coloring book and comic book #1; Mork & Mindy Na-No! Na-No! activity book and the official scrapbook.

Steve Van Antwerp — The Beverly Hillbillies paperback book; The Brady Bunch sticker fun book; Julia view-master; Patty Duke paperback book.

Bobbi Chamberlain — Little House on the Prairie lunch box; The Waltons lunch box.

PREFACE

This book has been in the making for several years. When we first started the hobby of collecting television memorabilia, we turned to collector books for assistance. We soon found that there was very little information on the subject. It was frustrating not knowing what items existed on our favorite shows or how much they were worth. As beginning collectors, we found ourselves paying too much for collectibles that were relatively common. At the same time, we passed up items that were scarce because we thought the prices were too high. After a few experiences like this, we realized the need for a collectible price guide to help us spend our money wisely. It was then that we committed ourselves to writing one.

We started by keeping an inventory of everything we purchased for our collection, including information on manufacturers, copyright years, prices paid, and what we believed to be the current values. We also kept a "want list" of other items we became aware of but didn't have in our collection.

Along with additional research and experience, we compiled this information into what we feel is the most comprehensive and accurate price guide directed solely toward collecting television memorabilia. Included in this book are collectibles from some of the most popular television shows from the '60s and '70s. We hope that this book will assist you in your collecting, whether you are just getting started or trying to complete a collection.

The authors are always interested in hearing from other collectors. If you have any comments or know of other memorabilia not contained in this guide, please write to:

Bill Morgan and Greg Davis
P. O. Box 11002
Whittier, CA 90603-0002
or
e-mail: tvtoys@aol.com

INTRODUCTION

Who would have ever thought that a single pack of Three's Company gum cards would have escalated into a collection of TV memorabilia consisting of over 5,000 items? Not us. But that is exactly what happened, and it seemed like it happened overnight.

There are several antique and collectible guide writers who describe collecting as the act of hunting for items to complete a collection. They theorize that humans are hunters by instinct. The Webster's Dictionary describes collecting as accumulating objects in one place. We, however, have a different definition. Instead of "completing a collection," we define it as "fulfilling an obsession." How else can we explain how rapidly our collection grew?

We recently showcased part of our collection at the Fullerton Museum in California. The exhibition was entitled "Gotta Have It: The Nature of Collecting." We soon realized we were not the only ones who found the act of collecting to be a very powerful and almost consuming inner force. The collectors that took part in the exhibit were from a variety of backgrounds. What we all had in common was the desire to fill a part of us that is comforted by the items we collect.

Our desire to collect TV memorabilia comes as no surprise. After all, we grew up during the '60s and '70s watching television. It was the perfect baby-sitter; always available and free. We remember waking up on Saturday mornings to tune into the classics of our time, like *Josie and the Pussycats, H. R. Pufnstuf, Sigmund and the Sea Monsters,* and *The Krofft Supershow.* Then, at night, when our homework was done, we would sit down and watch *The Love Boat, Fantasy Island, Laverne and Shirley, Little House on the Prairie, The Brady Bunch,* and *The Partridge Family.* Reruns of television shows from the '60s made it possible for us to enjoy *Bewitched, Gilligan's Island, I Dream of Jeannie,* and *The Beverly Hillbillies.* Watching all of these shows was comforting and dependable. We could always count on them to be there for our enjoyment.

Collecting TV memorabilia is like recapturing those same feelings. It's a return to a time when everything seemed safer, and we could take refuge from the world in our television set.

So, whether collecting TV memorabilia is an instinctive act or simply a way to recapture your childhood, one thing's for certain. It is extremely contagious. If you're just beginning, proceed with caution. Your one prized possession may very well grow into a room-filled obsession!

COLLECTIBLES INCLUDED IN THIS GUIDE

Television fans collect a number of different things, including autographs, magazine articles, and photographs of their favorite stars. In this guide, we have focused on items that were marketed for the purpose of promoting a television show during its original run. This would include toys, books, games, posters, school supplies, or other items that bear the name of the show. Although a lot of collectors include other items in their private collection, it would be cumbersome to list, for example, all of the magazine covers that Farrah Fawcett appeared on.

Due to the large number of magazines that celebrities have appeared on, and because they are very difficult to document, the only magazine included in this book is *TV Guide. TV Guide* is included because it is in itself a collectible about television. Its cover also features the cast or cast members credited as characters from the show.

A few records that have been included in this book do not bear the name of a television program. These recordings were made by actors or actresses during the original run of the show. These celebrities did not have an active singing career prior to the show or continue one after it ended. Most of these recordings were promoted by agents or pursued by merchandisers and are inadvertently television memorabilia.

PRICING

The intention of this price guide is to give a range of values to a comprehensive list of memorabilia made for each show. We have pulled together several resources to obtain as much information as possible regarding description and price. The values listed are approximate. As any experienced collector knows, prices are influenced by several factors. These include condition, rarity, popularity, and geographical location.

We feel one of the largest factors that can influence price is popularity. If there are several collectors focusing their hobby on one particular show, each may be willing to pay a premium to obtain an item to complete a collection. A collector may be willing to spend more, and a seller may be able to charge more for some items.

What we have tried to do is give over-all collectible prices. We have averaged the factors of rarity, popularity, and geographical location. The range of values have been estimated for items in excellent condition. If the object is above or below excellent condition, the collector should adjust the value accordingly.

10 RULES OF COLLECTING

1. Always trust your instincts. If you see an item you want and can afford it, don't pass it up. It may never come around again.

2. Understand the phrase "out-of-print." If you really want it, buy it. Remember, money is still being printed, but The Brady Bunch game hasn't been manufactured since 1973.

3. Always ask what the price is. Most toy dealers and traders are willing to negotiate prices, even if the price is marked. You can even ask if a dealer gives discounts when visiting an antique mall.

4. Don't pass up a collectible because it's not in mint condition. Mint items are scarce. Don't deny yourself the enjoyment of owning an item that you can up-grade later for one in better condition.

5. Have an inquiring mind. When searching for memorabilia, always ask sellers if they have any other items you're looking for. Just because you don't see it, doesn't mean they don't have it. You can also give out "want lists" to identify items you're seeking.

6. Know where to look. Make sure to visit garage sales, antique malls, record stores, thrift shops, antique swap meets, and used bookstores. You can also browse through publications devoted to buying and selling memorabilia.

7. Enlist family and friends for help. You can't be in all places at once, so having others keep a look-out for items you want can be invaluable.

8. Make friends with other collectors. Building a network of co-collectors can help you locate items you're looking for. You can also trade with one another.

9. Be organized. Keep track of what you have to avoid buying duplicates. This will also help you identify items missing from your collection so you can make want lists.

10. Have fun!

THE BEVERLY HILLBILLIES

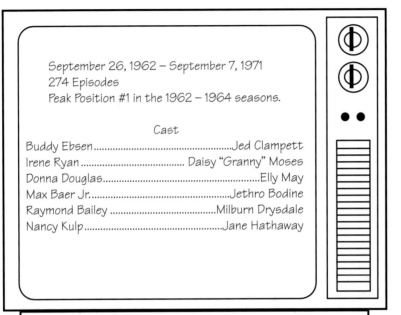

September 26, 1962 – September 7, 1971
274 Episodes
Peak Position #1 in the 1962 – 1964 seasons.

Cast

Buddy Ebsen.......................................Jed Clampett
Irene Ryan ....Daisy "Granny" Moses
Donna Douglas...Elly May
Max Baer Jr..Jethro Bodine
Raymond Bailey ....Milburn Drysdale
Nancy Kulp.....................................Jane Hathaway

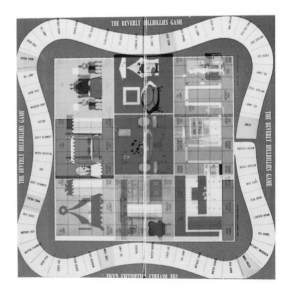

Above and right: BOARD GAME, Standard Toykraft, 1963.
$35.00 – $45.00.

BOOK, *The Saga of Wildcat Creek*, Whitman, 1966. $8.00 – $12.00.

BRITISH ANNUALS, World, 1964 – 1967. One for each year, except 1967 had two annuals: one with Granny, Elly May, and Jethro on cover; the other Granny, Elly May, and cougar. 1964 annual pictured. $30.00 – $35.00 each.

CARD GAME, Milton Bradley, 1963. $15.00 – $20.00.

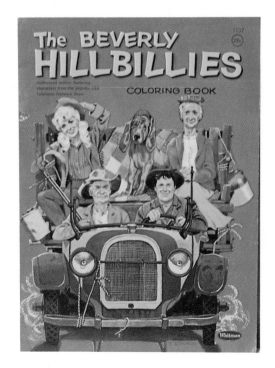

COLORING BOOK #1137, Whitman, 1963. $20.00 – $25.00.

CARTOON KIT, Colorforms, 1963. $50.00 – $75.00.

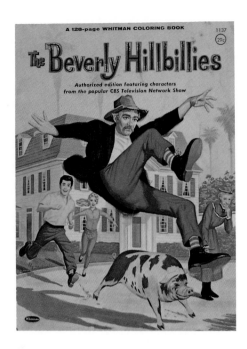

COLORING BOOK #1137, Whitman, 1963.
$20.00 – $25.00.

COLORING BOOK #1137, Whitman, 1964.
$20.00 – $25.00.

COMIC BOOKS #1-21, Dell, 1963 – 1971. #1, 10, 12, 14, 20, 21 pictured.
$25.00 – $50.00 #1. $10.00 – $15.00 each #2 – 21.

Right: DOLLS, Elly May Clampett, Unique, 1960s. Cereal premium mail-away. Two different versions. One has pants and the other a skirt. $50.00 – $75.00 each.

Above and right: FRAME TRAY PUZZLES, Jaymar, 1963.
Several different. $15.00 – $20.00 each.

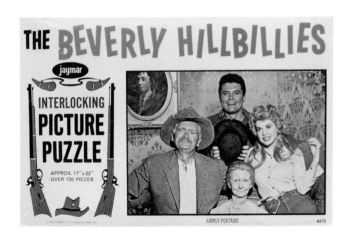

JIGSAW PUZZLES, Jaymar, 1963. Several different. Puzzle #6572 pictured. $15.00 – $20.00 each.

LUNCH BOX, Aladdin, 1963. Metal box with metal thermos.
$75.00 – $100.00 box. $40.00 – $50.00 thermos.

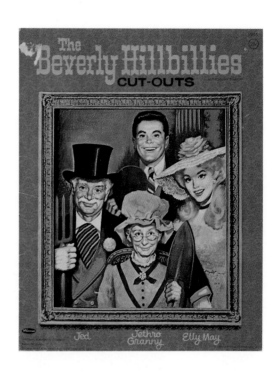

PAPER DOLL BOOKLET #1955, Whitman, 1964.
$50.00 – $75.00.

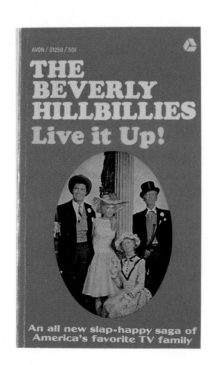

PAPERBACK BOOK, *The Beverly Hillbillies Live
It Up*, Avon Books, 1965. $8.00 – $10.00.

SONG BOOK, Alfred Music, 1963.
$20.00 – $25.00.

TRADING CARDS, Topps, 1963.
66 photo cards in set. Backs include Hillbilly Gags. 1¢
or 5¢ wrappers.

$350.00 – $500.00 set
$5.00 – $8.00 single cards
$50.00 – $75.00 1¢ wrapper
$125.00 – $150.00 5¢ wrapper
$200.00 – $250.00 display box.

VIEW-MASTER #B570, Sawyers, 1963.
$25.00 – $35.00.

TV GUIDES, 1962 – 1970.
11/10/62 Cast (not pictured); 03/09/63 Ebsen and Douglas;
09/07/63 Ryan and Douglas; 02/27/65 Hillbilly Women; 03/12/66
Cast illustrated; 07/11/70 Cast illustrated. $8.00 – $15.00 each.

Other items not pictured:

BEVERLY HILLBILLIES CAR, Ideal, 1963. Plastic car with figures. $300.00 – $500.00.

BOOK, *Granny's Hillbilly Cookbook*, Prentice Hall, 1966. Illustration of Granny wearing chef's hat. $10.00 – $15.00.

BUBBLE PIPE, Kellogg's Cereal, 1960s. Cereal premium. Bubbles created with water. $50.00 – $75.00.

HALLOWEEN COSTUME, Granny, Halco, 1971. $100.00 – $125.00.

HALLOWEEN COSTUME, Jed, Ben Cooper, 1963. $100.00 – $125.00.

HILLBILLY HAT, Tandy Leather Co., 1960s. Made of leather. $50.00 – $75.00.

HILLBILLY HAT, Arlington Hat Co., 1960s. Made of felt. $50.00 – $75.00.

MODEL KIT, Truck, MPC, 1968. $100.00 – $125.00.

PAPERBACK BOOK, *The Clampetts of Beverly Hills*, Avon Books, 1960s. $8.00 – $12.00.

PLASTIC PALETTE COLORING SET, Standard Toykraft, 1963. Illustration of cast on boxed set. Has ten pictures to color with crayons and eight paints. $50.00 – $75.00.

PUNCH OUT BOOK #1949, Whitman, 1964. Illustrated cast on cover. $50.00 – $75.00.

RECORD/LP, "The Beverly Hillbillies," Harmony, 1968. Photo cover of cast in their truck. Vocals by the cast. $35.00 – $45.00.

RECORD/LP, "Howdy," Reprise, 1965. Vocals by Buddy Ebsen. $15.00 – $20.00.

RECORD/45, "Mail Order Bride"/"Ballad of Jed Clampett," MGM, 1963. Vocals by Buddy Ebsen. Without picture sleeve. $5.00 – $8.00.

RECORD/45, "Howdy"/"Bonapart's Retreat," Reprise, 1965. Vocals by Buddy Ebsen. Without picture sleeve. $5.00 – $8.00.

RECORD/45, "Granny's Mini Skirt"/"Bring On the Show," Nashwood, 1972. Vocals by Irene Ryan. With picture sleeve. $15.00 – $20.00.

RECORD/45, "No Time at All"/"Time (To Believe in Each Other)," Motown, 1973. Vocals by Irene Ryan. Without picture sleeve. $5.00 – $8.00.

SHEET MUSIC, "Ballad of Jed Clampett," Carolintone Music, 1963. $15.00 – $20.00.

SLIDING SQUARES PUZZLE, Roalex, 1960s. Hand-held plastic puzzle with illustration of cast. $30.00 – $40.00.

TRU-VUE "MAGIC EYES" SET, 1960s. Viewer cards are rectangular in shape. Three cards come in a box. $50.00 – $75.00.

BEWITCHED

September 17, 1964 – July 1, 1972
252 Episodes
Peak Position: #2 in the 1964 – 1965 season.

Cast

Elizabeth Montgomery ....Samantha Stevens/Serena
Dick York/Dick Sargent.............................Darrin Stevens
Agnes Moorehead ....Endora
David White...Larry Tate
Irene Vernon/Kasey Rogers ....Louise Tate
Erin/Diane Murphy ....Tabitha
David/Greg Lawrence ....Adam
Alice Pearce/Sandra Gould ....Gladys Kravitz
George Tobias..................................... Abner Kravitz

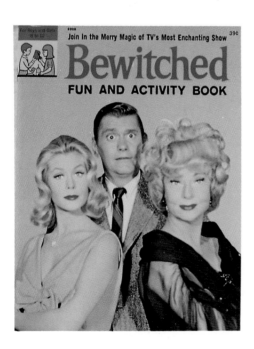

ACTIVITY BOOK, Treasure, 1965.
$15.00 – $20.00.

BOOK, *The Opposite Uncle*, Whitman, 1970.
$10.00 – $15.00.

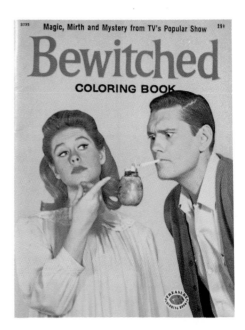

BRITISH ANNUALS, World, 1967 – 1968.
$25.00 – $35.00 each.

COLORING BOOK, Treasure, 1965.
$25.00 – $35.00.

CARD GAME, Stymie, Milton Bradley, 1965.
$25.00 – $30.00.

COMIC BOOKS
#1 – 14, Dell, 1965 – 1969.
#'s 1 and 14 not pictured.
$25.00 – $50.00 #1
$15.00 – $30.00 #2 – 14.

PAPERBACK BOOK, Bewitched,
Dell, 1965. $10.00 – $15.00.

DOLL, Samantha, Ideal, 1966. Original packaging includes
window box and broom.
$125.00 – $175.00 loose. $400.00 – $500.00 boxed.

PAPER DOLL BOX, Samanatha, Magic Wand,
1965. $75.00 – $100.00.

STORY BOOK, Wonder Books, 1965.
$15.00 – $20.00.

WRITING TABLET, 1960s. $20.00 – $25.00.

TV GUIDES, 1964 – 1970.
11/28/64 Montgomery (not pictured); 05/29/65 Montgomery and
York; 6/18/66 Cast (not pictured); 05/13/67 Montgomery;
01/27/68 Montgomery; 03/22/69 Montgomery; 02/07/70 Montgomery and Sargent illustrated. $8.00 – $15.00 each.

Other items not pictured:

BEWITCHED BROOM, Amsco, 1965. $100.00 – $125.00.

BOARD GAME, The Samantha and Endora Game, Game Gems, 1965.
$40.00 – $60.00.

DOLL, Tabitha, Ideal, 1966. Marketed as "Tabatha." $125.00 – $150.00.

HALLOWEEN COSTUME, Samantha, Ben Cooper, 1965. $100.00 – 125.00.

HI-CHAIR FEEDING SET, Amsco, 1965. $150.00 – $200.00.

JIGSAW PUZZLES, Along For the Ride and Endora Pours, Milton Bradley, 1964. Both come with a
Samantha photo insert. $40.00 – $60.00 each.

MAGIC COFFEE SET, Amsco, 1965. $150.00 – $200.00.

MAGIC FEEDING BOTTLE, Amsco, 1965. $50.00 – $75.00.

MAGIC FEEDING BOTTLE SET, Amsco, 1965. With vinyl travel bag. $150.00 – $200.00.

PAPER DOLL BOX, Tabitha, Magic Wand, 1965. $50.00 – $75.00.

PLAY DISHES, 1968. Plastic dishes for play with Tabitha doll. $75.00 – $100.00.

SHEET MUSIC, Theme, 1964. Cover photo of Darrin, Samantha, and Endora.
$30.00 – $40.00.

TRADING CARDS, Topps, 1960s. Test issue of 28 cards. Black and white photo cards with blank
backs. They are not numbered. $100.00 – $150.00 single cards.

THE BIONIC WOMAN

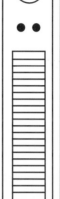

January 14, 1976 – September 2, 1978
57 Episodes
Peak Position: #5 in the 1975 – 1976 season.

Cast

Lindsay Wagner..Jaime Sommers
Richard Anderson.......................................Oscar Goldman
Martin E. Brooks...Dr. Rudy Wells
Jennifer Darling...Peggy Callahan

ACRYLIC PAINT BY NUMBER SET, Craft Master, 1976.
$15.00 – $20.00.

ACTIVITY BOOK, Action-Adventure Activity Book,
Grosset & Dunlap, 1976. $8.00 – $10.00.

ACTIVITY BOOK, Fun Activity Book, Grosset & Dunlap, 1976. $8.00 – $10.00.

BIONIC EYEWEAR, Hudson, 1977. Fabric eyeglass case. $10.00 – $15.00.

BIONIC TATTOOS & STICKERS, Kenner, 1976. $8.00 – $12.00.

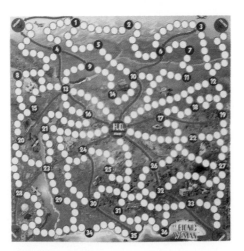

Above and right: BOARD GAME, Parker Brothers, 1976. $10.00 – $15.00.

BRITISH ANNUALS, Brown Watson, 1978 – 1979.
$15.00 – $20.00 each.

CARRIAGE HOUSE, Kenner, 1977. Playset
for the 12" dolls. $75.00 – $100.00.

COLORING BOOK, The Bionic Woman Colouring Book,
Stafford Pemberton, 1977, European. $10.00 – $15.00.

COLORING BOOK, Adventure Coloring Book, Treasure Books, 1976. $8.00 – $10.00.

COLORING BOOK, Goodtime Coloring Book, Treasure Books, 1977. $8.00 – $10.00.

COLORING BOOK, Coloring Fun Book, Treasure Books, 1976. $8.00 – $10.00.

COMIC BOOKS #1 – 5, Charlton, 1977 – 1978. $3.00 – $5.00 each.

CUP AND TUMBLER, Dawn, 1976.
$8.00 – 12.00 each.

DIP DOTS, Kenner, 1977. $15.00 – $20.00.

DOLL, Fembot, Kenner, 1977.
$40.00 – $60.00.

DOLLS, Jaime Sommers, Kenner, 1976. Two versions. One comes with a mission purse. $30.00 – $45.00 each.

DOLL FASHIONS, Kenner, 1976. Several different. "Red Dazzle" pictured. $10.00 – $15.00 each.

GIVE-A-SHOW PROJECTOR, Kenner, 1977. $20.00 – $25.00.

HALLOWEEN COSTUME, Jaime, Ben Cooper, 1975.
$10.00 – $15.00.

JIGSAW PUZZLES, APC, 1976. Several different boxed versions. #1485 pictured.
$8.00 – 12.00 each.

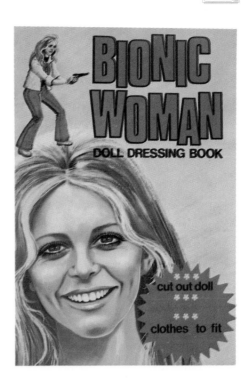

PAPER DOLL BOOKLET,
Stafford Pemberton,
1978, European.
$20.00 – $25.00.

JIGSAW PUZZLES, APC, 1976. Four
different canister illustrations. #1245
pictured. $8.00 – $12.00 each.

Right and below: LUNCH BOXES, Aladdin, 1977 – 1978.
Two versions of boxes and thermoses exist. Both boxes
have identical fronts. One has Jaime opening car door
on back (1977) and the other shows her running with
the bionic dog (1978). Metal box with plastic thermos.
$25.00 – $30.00 each box
$10.00 – $15.00 each thermos.

PAPERBACK BOOK, *Brain Teasers*, Tempo Books, 1976. $5.00 – $8.00.

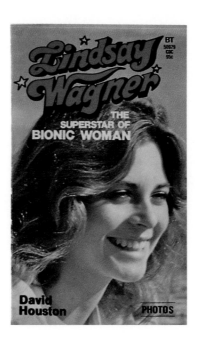

PAPERBACK BOOK, *Lindsay Wagner: Superstar of the Bionic Woman*, Belmont Tower Books, 1976. $5.00 – $8.00.

PAPERBACK BOOK, *The Bionic Woman: A Question of Life*, Star, 1977, European. $8.00 – $12.00.

PAPERBACK BOOKS, *Welcome Home, Jaime* and *Extracurricular Activities*, Berkely, 1976 – 1977. $3.00 – $5.00 each.

PLAY SUIT, Ben Cooper, 1975. Fabric costume with plastic mask. $25.00 – $30.00.

PLAY-DOH ACTION PLAY SET, Kenner, 1977. $15.00 – $20.00.

RECORD/LP, "Great Adventures," Wonderland, 1976.
Narrated stories. $10.00 – $15.00.

SEE-A-SHOW VIEWER, Kenner, 1976.
$10.00 – $15.00.

STYLING BOUTIQUE, Kenner, 1977.
$35.00 – $45.00.

WALLET, Faberge, 1976.
Blue or pink. European.
$15.00 – $20.00.

TV GUIDES, 1976 – 1978.
05/08/76 Wagner; 05/18/78 Wagner
$5.00 – $8.00 each.

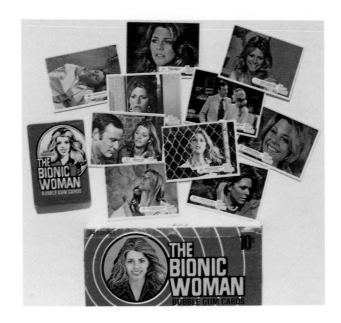

TRADING CARDS, Donruss, 1976. 44 photo cards in set with puzzle backs.
$20.00 – $25.00 set. $.50 – $.75 single cards.
$3.00 – $5.00 wrapper. $15.00 – $20.00 display box.

Other items not pictured:

BANK, Animals Plus, 1976. 10" plastic figural. $10.00 – $15.00.

BEAUTY SALON, Kenner, 1976. Play set for 12" dolls. $25.00 – $30.00.

DOME HOUSE, Kenner, 1977. Inflatable doll house for 12" dolls. $40.00 – $60.00.

LUNCH BOX, 1970s. Plastic version from Canada with same illustration as metal box.
$25.00 – $30.00 box; $10.00 – $15.00 thermos.

MODEL KIT, Bionic Repair Kit, MPC, 1978. $25.00 – $30.00.

MOVIE VIEWER, Kenner, 1977. Hand-held viewer for movie cassettes. $25.00 – $30.00.

MOVIE VIEWER CASSETTES, Kenner, 1977. Several different in numbered boxes sold
separately for movie viewer. $10.00 – $15.00 each.

PAPER DOLL PLAYSET, 1970s. Bionic Woman and Six Million Dollar Man cutouts in
box, European. $40.00 – $50.00.

PAPERBACK BOOK, *The Bionic Woman: Double Indemnity*, Star, 1977. European.
$8.00 – $12.00.

SPORTS CAR, Kenner, 1977. Vehicle in box for 12" doll. $40.00 – $60.00.

TOOTHBRUSH, 1970s. Battery-operated. $25.00 – $35.00.

TOWER AND CYCLE, Kenner, 1977. Motorcycle with jumping action. $25.00 – $30.00.

WRISTWATCH, MZ Berger, 1970s. Working watch with illustration of Jaime.
$50.00 – $75.00.

THE BRADY BUNCH

September 26, 1969 – August 30, 1974
117 Episodes
Peak Position: Not in the top 25.
September 16, 1972 – August 31, 1974
22 Episodes of The Brady Kids animated cartoon.

Cast

Robert Reed.. Mike
Florence Henderson .... Carol
Barry Williams ....Greg
Maureen McCormick ....Marcia
Chris Knight..Peter
Eve Plumb...Jan
Mike Lookinland..Bobby
Susan Olsen...Cindy
Ann B. Davis..Alice

ACTIVITY BOOK #1252, Whitman, 1974.
$20.00 – $25.00.

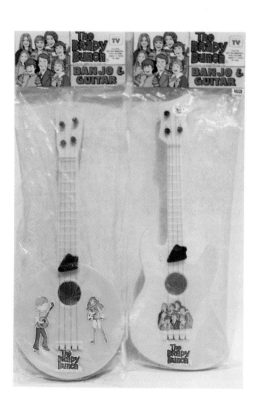

BANJO AND GUITAR, Larami, 1973.
$25.00 – $30.00 each.

Left and below: BOARD GAME, Whitman, 1973.
$100.00 – $125.00.

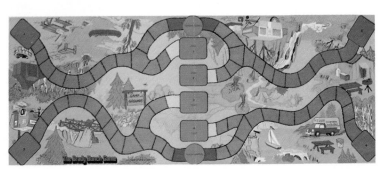

BRAIN TWISTERS, Larami, 1973. $20.00 – $25.00.

CIGAR BANDS, 1970s. European set of 12.
$75.00 – $100.00.

COLORING BOOK #1004, Whitman, 1974. $20.00 – $25.00.

COLORING BOOK #1035, Whitman, 1972. $20.00 – $25.00.

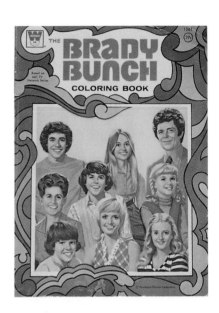

COLORING BOOK #1061, Whitman, 1973. $20.00 – $25.00.

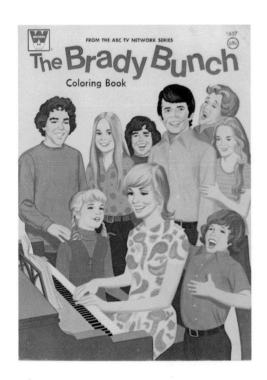

COLORING BOOK #1657, Whitman, 1974. $20.00 – $25.00.

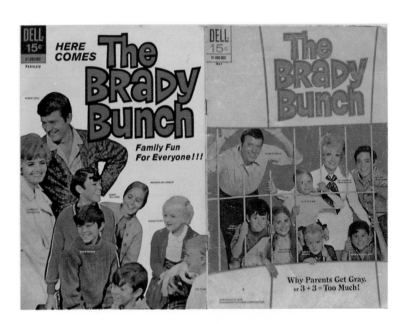

COMIC BOOKS #1 – 2, Dell, 1970. $30.00 – $40.00 each.

FISHIN' FUN SET, Larami, 1973.
$20.00 – $25.00.

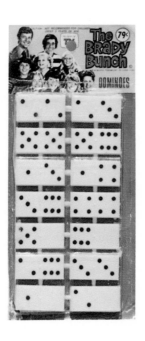

DOMINOES, Larami, 1973.
$20.00 – $25.00.

FRAME TRAY PUZZLE, Whitman, 1972.
$35.00 – $45.00.

HALLOWEEN COSTUME, Greg. Costume says "One of
the Brady Bunch," but "Greg" is printed on box, Collegeville, 1970s. $40.00 – $50.00.

HEX-A-GAME, Larami, 1973.
$20.00 – $25.00.

KITE FUN BOOK, Western Publishing Co., 1976.
$20.00 – $25.00.

LUNCH BOX, K.S.T., 1969. Metal box with metal thermos.
$125.00 – $175.00 box. $35.00 – $50.00 thermos.

OUTDOOR FUN SETS, Larami, 1973. 4 different. Slide set not pictured. $20.00 – $25.00 each.

PAPER DOLL BOOKLETS #1976 and
#1997, Whitman, 1973. Two different ver-
sions. White version has pool inside and
orange version has no pool.
$25.00 – $35.00 each.

PAPER DOLL BOX #4784/7418,
Whitman, 1972. $30.00 – $40.00.

PAPER DOLL BOX #4320/7209,
Whitman, 1973. $30.00 – $40.00.

PAPER DOLL BOX #4340/7420,
Whitman, 1974. $30.00 – $40.00.

PAPERBACK BOOKS #1–5, Lancer,
1969 – 1970.
  $15.00 – $20.00 each #'s 2 and 4
  $5.00 – $10.00 each #1, 3, and 5.

PAPERBACK BOOKS, Tiger Beat, 1972 – 1973. *The Treasure of Mystery Island, The New York Mystery, and Adventures On the High Seas.* $5.00 – $8.00 each.

RECORD/LP, "Merry Christmas From the Brady Bunch," Paramount, 1971. $50.00 – $75.00.

RECORD/LP, "Meet the Brady Bunch," Paramount, 1972. $25.00 – $30.00.

RECORD/LP, "The Kids From the Brady Bunch," Paramount, 1972. $25.00 – $30.00.

RECORD/LP, "Phonographic Album," Paramount, 1973.
$25.00 – $30.00.

RECORD/LP, "Chris Knight & Maureen McCormick," Paramount,
1973. $40.00 – $60.00.

RECORD/45, "Frosty the Snowman"/"Silver Bells," Paramount,
1971. $20.00 – $25.00.

RECORD/45, "Zuckerman's Famous Pig"/"Charlotte's Web," Paramount, 1973. Back features square photos of the Brady kids.
$20.00 – $25.00.

RECORD/45, "Love Doesn't Care Who's In It"/"Gum Drop," Capitol Records, 1973. Vocals by Mike Lookinland. $20.00 – $25.00.

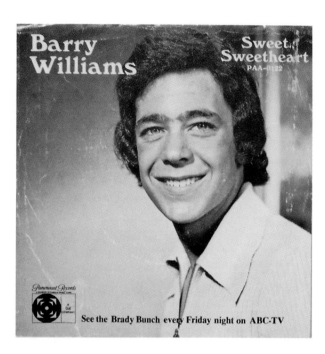

RECORD/45, "Sweet Sweetheart"/"Sunny," Paramount, 1973. Vocals by Barry Williams. $20.00 – $25.00.

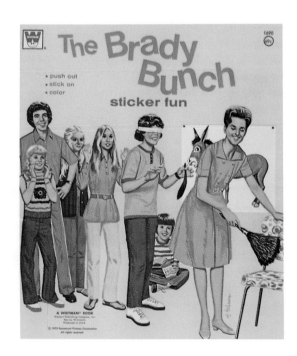

STICKER FUN BOOK, Whitman, 1973. $40.00 – $50.00.

SHEET MUSIC, "(I'm a) Yo Yo Man," Martin Cooper Music, 1973. $30.00 – $40.00.

VIEW-MASTER #B568, Grand Canyon Adventure, GAF, 1971. $25.00 – $30.00.

TALKING VIEW-MASTER #AVB568, Grand Canyon Adventure, GAF, 1971. $30.00 – $35.00.

TV GUIDE.
4/4/70. $15.00 – $20.00.

TRADING CARDS, Topps, 1969. 88 cards in set with puzzle backs. Released in 1971.
$600.00 – $800.00 set. $6.00 – $10.00 single cards.
$60.00 – $75.00 wrapper. $300.00 – $400.00 display box.

Other items not pictured:

BOOKLETS, *Chris Knight's Photo Album* and *The Secret of Chris Knight*, Tiger Beat, 1972. $10.00 – $15.00 each.

CHESS AND CHECKERS SET, Larami, 1973. Window box with photo of cast. $20.00 – $25.00.

DOLL, Kitty-Carry-All, Remco, 1969. $100.00 – $125.00.

FAN CLUB KIT, Tiger Beat, 1972. Fan kit contains a personal message record, book of Brady facts, autographed portraits, stickers, membership card, and wallet photos. $150.00 – $200.00.

HALLOWEEN COSTUME, Marcia, 1970s. $100.00 – $125.00.

HAND TAMBOURINE, Larami, 1973. On card with illustration of cast. $20.00 – $25.00.

JUMP ROPE, Larami, 1973. $20.00 – $25.00.

MAGIC SLATE, Larami, 1973. Illustration of cast. $30.00 – $35.00.

PAPERBACK BOOK, *Every Girl Can Be Popular*, by Maureen McCormick. Tiger Beat, 1972. $15.00 – $20.00.

PURSE, Larami, 1973. $20.00 – $25.00.

RECORD/45, Paramount, 1973. "Over and Over"/"Good For Each Other." With fold-out picture sleeve. Vocals by Chris Knight. $20.00 – $25.00.

RECORD/45, RCA, 1970s. "The Fortune Cookie Song"/"How Will It Be." Without picture sleeve. Vocals by Eve Plumb. $10.00 – $15.00.

RECORDS/45's, Paramount, 1972–73. "We'll Always Be Friends"/"Time to Change"; "I'd Love You to Want Me"/"Everything I Do"; "Candy Sugar Shop"/"Drummer Man"; "Time to Change"/"We Can Make the World a Whole Lot Brighter." Without picture sleeves. $10.00 – $15.00 each.

RECORDS/45's, Paramount, 1972 – 1973. "Little Bird"/"Just Singin' Alone"; "Love's in the Roses"/"Harmonize"; "Truckin' Back to You"/"Teeny Weeny Bit Too Long." Without picture sleeves. Vocals by Maureen McCormick. $10.00 – $15.00.

TOY GROCERIES, Larami, 1973. Window box with illustration of cast. $20.00 – $25.00.

TOY TEA SET, Larami, 1973. On card with illustration of the Brady girls. $20.00 – $25.00.

TRADING CARDS, Topps. 1970. 55 cards in test set. Identical to the first 55 cards of the 1969 set except they bear the 1970 copyright on back. $20.00 – $25.00 single cards. $1,200.00 – $1,500.00 set.

THE BUGALOOS

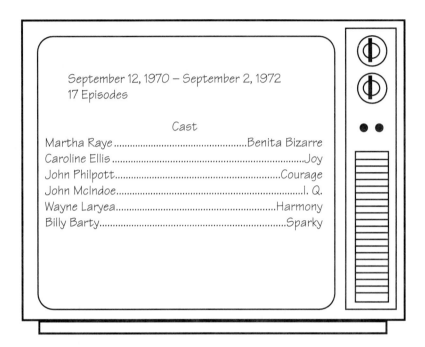

September 12, 1970 – September 2, 1972
17 Episodes

Cast

Martha Raye...Benita Bizarre
Caroline Ellis ....Joy
John Philpott..Courage
John McIndoe...I. Q.
Wayne Laryea...Harmony
Billy Barty..Sparky

Above and right: BOARD GAME, Milton Bradley, 1971.
$30.00 – $40.00.

COMIC BOOKS #1 – 4, Charlton, 1971 – 1972. #2 not pictured.
$15.00 – $20.00 each.

LUNCH BOX, Aladdin, 1971. Metal box with plastic thermos.
$40.00 – $50.00 box. $20.00 – $25.00 thermos.

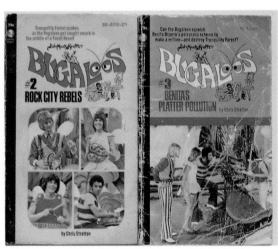

PAPERBACK BOOKS #1 – 3, Curtis Books, 1971. #1 not pictured. $15.00 – $20.00 each.

RECORD/LP, "The Bugaloos," Capitol Records, 1970. $25.00 – $30.00.

RECORD/45, "For a Friend"/"The Senses of Our World," Capitol Records, 1971. Two different versions. One released in Japan with a picture sleeve and one in the U.S. without a picture sleeve. Japanese import pictured. $25.00 – $30.00 import; $5.00 – $10.00 domestic.

Other items not pictured:

CIGAR BANDS, 1970s. European set of 12. $50.00 – $75.00.

CUT N' PASTE BOOK, Whitman, 1971. Illustrated cover. $30.00 – $40.00.

HALLOWEEN COSTUME, Joy, Ben Cooper, 1971. $40.00 – $60.00.

CHARLIE'S ANGELS

September 22, 1976 – August 19, 1981
115 Episodes
Peak Position: #4 in the 1977 – 1978 season.

Cast

Kate Jackson ....Sabrina Duncan

Jaclyn Smith .... Kelly Garrett

Farrah Fawcett...Jill Munroe

Cheryl Ladd ....Kris Munroe

Shelley Hack ....Tiffany Wells

Tanya Roberts..Julie Rogers

David Doyle..John Bosley

John Forsythe ....Charles Townsend

3-D VIEWER, Fleetwood, 1977, $15.00 – $20.00.

ADVENTURE VAN, Hasbro, 1978. Play van for the 8½"
dolls. $40.00 – $50.00.

BEAUTY PRODUCTS, Farrah, Faberge, 1970s. Shampoo, conditioner, hair spray, soap, and deodorant. Conditioner pictured. $10.00 – $15.00 each.

ANGELS' BEADS, Fleetwood, 1977. Sets vary with background photos of Sabrina, Kelly, Kris, and Jill. Jewelry comes with logo, Charlie's Angels or Sabrina, Kelly, Kris. $15.00 – $20.00 each.

BEAUTY SETS, Fleetwood, 1977. Sets vary with photos of Sabrina, Kelly, Kris, and Jill. Plastic comb and mirror come in different colors. $10.00 – $15.00 each.

Above and right: BOARD GAME, Milton Bradley, 1977. Features Jill. $10.00 – $15.00.

Above and right: BOARD GAME, Milton Bradley, 1978. Features Kris.
$10.00 – $15.00.

BOOKLET Farrah, Kate and Jaclyn –
An Unauthorized Biography, 1970s.
$10.00 – $15.00.

BRITISH ANNUALS, Stafford Pemberton, 1978 – 1981. 1981 annual featuring Tiffany is not pictured. $15.00 – $20.00 each.

BRUNCH BAG, Aladdin, 1977. Vinyl bag with plastic thermos.
$50.00 – $75.00 bag. $10.00 – $15.00 thermos.

COLORFORMS ADVENTURE SET, Colorforms, 1978. $30.00 – $40.00.

BUTTONS, Farrah, 1970s. $8.00 – $12.00 each.

CORGI VANS, Mettoy, 1977.
$20.00 – $25.00 3". $30.00 – $35.00 5".

COSMETIC BEAUTY KIT, H. G. Toys, 1977. $50.00 – $75.00.

CUPS, MUGS, AND TUMBLERS,
Farrah, Thermo-Serv, 1977.
Matching set for each of three
styles. $10.00 – $20.00 each.

CUPS, MUGS, AND TUMBLERS, Thermo-Serv,
1977. Matching set for Sabrina, Kelly, and
Kris. Kelly mug and tumbler pictured.
$15.00 – $25.00 each.

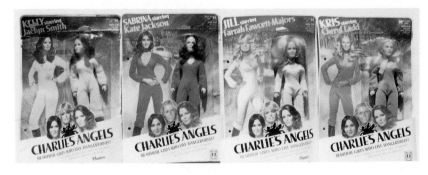

DOLLS, Kelly, Sabrina, Jill, and Kris, Hasbro, 1977. 8½" dolls. Also sold as gift set in
one box. One version with Jill and another with Kris.
$20.00 – $25.00 each. $75.00 – $100.00 gift set.

DOLLS, Cheryl Ladd and Kate Jackson, Mattel, 1978. 12" dolls.
$30.00 – $45.00 each.

DOLLS, Farrah and Jaclyn Smith, Mego, 1977. 12" dolls.
$30.00 – $45.00 each.

DOLL, Farrah, OK Toys, 1970s.
12" doll sold in plastic package.
Bathing suit or dress color
varies. $20.00 – $25.00.

DOLL, Farrah, Mego, 1980.
12" doll. $35.00 – $50.00.

DOLL OUTFITS, Farrah, Mego, 1977.
Several styles in boxes and on cards
for the 12" doll. Boxed Easy Living version pictured. $20.00 – $25.00 each.

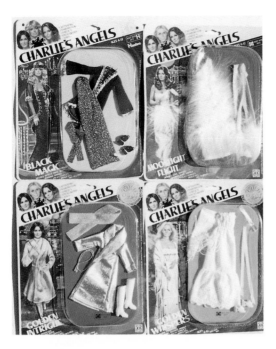

DOLL OUTFITS, Hasbro, 1977. Several different styles on cards for the 8½" dolls. $10.00 – $15.00 each.

DOLL OUTFITS AND ACTION GEAR, Hasbro, 1977. Set of three illustrated window boxes for the Jill, Kelly, and Sabrina 8½" dolls. $15.00 – $20.00 each.

DOLL OUTFIT, Jill's Flying Skateboard Adventure, Hasbro, 1977. For the 8½" doll. $15.00 – $20.00.

DRESSER SETS, Fleetwood, 1977. Sets vary with photos of Sabrina, Kelly, Kris, and Jill. Plastic comb, brush, and mirror came in different colors. $10.00 – $15.00 each.

FAN CLUB KIT, Cheryl Ladd, FCCA, 1979. $30.00 – $40.00.

FASHION TOTE, Hasbro, 1978. Carrying case for 8½" dolls and outfits. $15.00 – $20.00.

FAN CLUB KIT, Farrah, FCCA, 1978. $50.00 – $60.00.

GOLDEN ALL-STAR BOOK, Golden Press, 1977. Illustrated story book. $8.00 – $10.00.

FARRAH'S DRESSING ROOM PLAYSET, Mego, 1977. For the 12" doll. $50.00 – $75.00.

HAIR DRYER, Fleetwood, 1977.
$15.00 – $20.00.

HIDE-A-WAY HOUSE PLAYSET, Hasbro, 1978. Playset
for the 8½" dolls. $75.00 – $100.00.

HALLOWEEN COSTUME, Farrah, Collegeville, 1977.
$25.00 – $35.00.

HALLOWEEN COSTUME, Charlie's Angels, Collegeville,
1976. Box labeled as Charlie's Angels but mask
resembles Sabrina. $50.00 – $75.00.

JEWELRY SET, Fleetwood, 1977.
$15.00 – $20.00.

JEWELS AND CASE, Fleetwood, 1977.
$15.00 – $20.00.

JIGSAW PUZZLE, HG Toys,
1976. Giant-size with 250
pieces. $20.00 – $30.00.

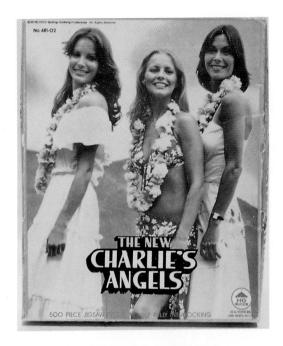

JIGSAW PUZZLE, HG Toys, 1977. 500 pieces.
$10.00 – $15.00.

JIGSAW PUZZLES, Farrah, APC, 1977, 200 and 405-piece sizes. One 405-piece size and three different styles for 200-piece sizes. 200-piece Farrah in T-top without flower not pictured. $15.00 – $25.00 each.

JIGSAW PUZZLES, HG Toys, 1976. Six different styles. #435-05 and 435-06 not pictured. $10.00 – $15.00 each.

LUNCH BOX, Aladdin, 1978. Metal box with plastic thermos. $25.00 – $35.00 box. $10.00 – $15.00 thermos.

LUGGAGE SETS, Travel Toy, 1977. 3-piece sets. Two different versions. One features Jill and the other features Kris. $40.00 – $60.00 each.

MODEL KIT, Charlie's Angels Van, Revell, 1977. Snap-together kit at 1/32 scale. Box features Kelly, Kris, and Sabrina. $20.00 – $30.00.

MIRROR, Lightline, 1977. $75.00 – $100.00.

MODEL KIT, Mobile Unit Van, Revell, 1977. 1/25 scale.
Box features Kelly, Jill, and Sabrina. $30.00 – $40.00.

MODEL KIT, Farrah's Foxy Vette, AMT, 1977. $30.00 – $40.00.

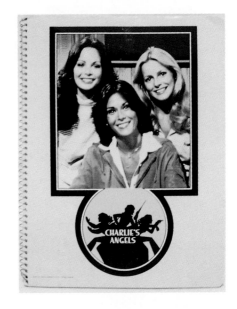

NOTEBOOKS, Stuart Hall, 1977. Different
cover photos of cast. $15.00 – $20.00 each.

NOTEBOOKS, Farrah, Poster Books, 1977. 3 different
styles. Farrah in T-top with and without flower not pictured.
$15.00 – $20.00 each.

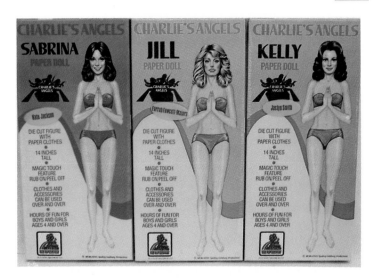

PAPER DOLLS, Sabrina, Jill, and Kelly, Toy Factory, 1977. $20.00 – $30.00 each.

PAINT BY NUMBERS SET, Hasbro, 1978. Set of two pictures with six acrylic paints. Box features illustration of Kelly, Kris, and Sabrina. $30.00 – $40.00.

PAPERBACK BOOKS #1–5, Ballantine, 1977 – 1978. $5.00 – $10.00 each.

PAPERBACK BOOK, Traver's Favorite Angels, Xerox, 1978. $8.00 – $10.00.

PAPERBACK BOOKS, Farrah's World, Dell, 1977; Farrah and Lee, Tempo, 1977; Farrah: An Unauthorized Biography, Signet, 1977. $5.00 – $8.00 each.

PENDANTS, Fleetwood, 1977. One for each character. Kris not pictured. $10.00 – $15.00 each.

PILLOWS, Farrah, Zodiac, 1977. Three different styles. Farrah in T-top with and without flower not pictured. $35.00 – $45.00 each.

POSTER ART KIT. Board King, 1977. Features Kelly, Jill, and Sabrina. Contains two posters and five markers. $25.00 – $35.00.

POSTER ART KIT, HG Toys, 1977. Features Kelly, Kris, and Sabrina. Contains two posters and five markers. $25.00 – $35.00.

POSTER PUT-ONS, Bi-Rite, 1977. Several different styles to match various posters. $8.00 – $10.00 each.

POSTERS, 1970s. Different styles featuring Jaclyn, Cheryl, Farrah, Kate, and group shots.
Several others not pictured. $15.00 – $25.00 each.

SABRINA OF CHARLIE'S ANGELS

CHERYL LADD as KRIS of CHARLIE'S ANGELS

KELLY OF CHARLIE'S ANGELS

PURSE, Farrah, Vanidades,
1970s. $30.00 – $40.00.

RECORD/45, "You"/"Let Me Get To Know You," KT Productions,
1977. Vocals by J.P. Vigon and Farrah Fawcett. $35.00 – $45.00.

RECORDS/45's, Cheryl Ladd, Capitol, 1970s. Several different with
picture sleeves.
    $5.00 – $10.00 each domestic. $15.00 – $20.00 each import.

RECORD/LP, "Cheryl Ladd," Capitol, 1978.
$10.00 – $15.00.

RECORD/LP, "Cheryl Ladd — Dance Forever," Capitol, 1979, $10.00 – $15.00.

SHEET MUSIC, "Cheryl Ladd — Think It Over," Kengorus Music, 1978. $8.00 – $10.00.

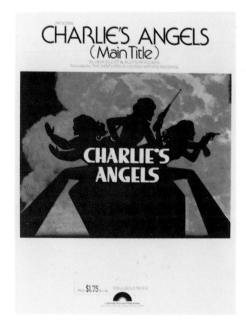

SHEET MUSIC, "Charlie's Angels (main title)," Columbia, 1977. $10.00 – $15.00.

SHOULDER BAG, Fleetwood, 1977. $15.00 – $20.00.

STYLING CENTERS, Farrah, Mego, 1977. Regular and grow-hair.
$30.00 – $40.00 each.

SUNGLASSES, Fleetwood, 1977. Sun-glasses and case. $15.00 – $20.00.

TALK-TIME TELEPHONE, Fleetwood,
1977. $15.00 – $20.00.

TARGET SET, Placo Toys, 1977. $40.00 – $50.00.

TOY FASHION WATCH, GLJ Toys, 1977.
$35.00 – $45.00.

TRADING CARDS SET #1, Topps, 1977. 55 cards and 11 stickers in set. Trivia and puzzle backs. Features Sabrina, Kelly, and Jill.

$35.00 – $45.00 set.	$.35 – $.50 single cards.
$.75 – $1.00 single stickers.	$5.00 – $8.00 wrapper.
$20.00 – $25.00 display box.	

TRADING CARDS SET #2, Topps, 1977. 66 cards and 11 stickers in set. Trivia and puzzle backs. Features Sabrina, Kelly, and Jill.

$35.00 – $45.00 set.	$.35 – $.50 single cards.
$.75 – $1.00 single stickers.	$5.00 – $8.00 wrapper.
$15.00 – $20.00 display box.	

TRADING CARDS SET #3, Topps, 1977. 66 cards and 11 stickers in set. Trivia and puzzle backs. Features Sabrina, Kelly, and Kris.
$25.00 – $35.00 set. $.25 – $.45 single cards.
$.50 – $.75 single stickers. $3.00 – $5.00 wrapper.
$10.00 – $15.00 display box.

TRADING CARDS SET #4, Topps, 1977. 66 cards and 11 stickers in set. Trivia and puzzle backs. Features Sabrina, Kelly, and Kris.
$25.00 – $35.00 set. $.25 – $.45 single cards.
$.50 – $.75 single stickers. $3.00 – $5.00 wrapper.
$10.00 – $15.00 display box.

TV GUIDES, 1976 – 1979.
09/25/76 Smith, Fawcett, and Jackson; 05/21/77 Fawcett; 02/18/78 Smith, Ladd, and Jackson; 08/26/78 Ladd; 12/29/79 Smith, Ladd, and Hack
$8.00 – $15.00 each.

VENDING MACHINE JEWELRY DISPLAY, The Real Faucet, 1970s. Plastic faucet keychains and necklaces. $35.00 – $45.00.

WALLET, Travel Toy, 1977. $20.00 – $25.00.

Other items not pictured:

BACKPACK, Travel Toy, 1977. Vinyl backpack featuring group photo of Kris, Kelly, and Sabrina on top flap. $50.00 – $75.00.

BEAN BAG CHAIRS, Farrah, 1977. Different styles. $60.00 – $80.00 each.

BEAUTY HAIR CARE SET, HG Toys, 1977. Boxed set comes with plastic dryer, brush, rollers, and photo bag featuring Kris, Kelly, and Sabrina. $50.00 – $75.00.

BELT BUCKLES, Farrah 1977. Two different styles. One with color photo of Farrah and the other a dripping faucet. $25.00 – $30.00 each.

BICYCLE, Huffy, 1970s. Angel logo on seat. $100.00 – $150.00.

BOOK, _Kate Jackson_, EMC Corp., 1970s. Hardback book with cover photo of Sabrina. $20.00 – $25.00.

CALENDAR, Farrah, 1978. $20.00 – $25.00.

CALENDARS, Roadshow, 1980 – 1981. Both featuring Kelly, Kris, and Tiffany. $20.00 – $25.00 each.

CHIFFON SCARF, Farrah, 1970s. $25.00 – $35.00.

CHILDREN'S BOOK, _It Takes a Thief_, Stafford Pemberton, 1970s. Illustration of Kelly, Kris, and Sabrina. European. $25.00 – $30.00.

CIGARETTE LIGHTERS, 1970s. Photos of individual characters. $20.00 – $25.00 each.

CLOTH CALENDAR, 1978. Featuring photo of Kelly, Kris, and Sabrina. $25.00 – $30.00.

COLORING BOOK, Stafford Pemberton, 1970s. Illustration of Kelly, Kris, and Sabrina. European. $35.00 – $45.00.

CUBEMENSIONAL PUZZLE, Sharin Toy Co., 1970s. $35.00 – $45.00.

DENIM JEANS, Azoulay, 1970s. Bell-bottom jeans with logo on back pocket. $30.00 – $40.00.

DOLL OUTFITS, Kate Jackson and Cheryl Ladd, Mattel, 1978. Various outfits on cards for the 12" dolls. $10.00 – $15.00 each.

FACIAL TISSUE, Farrah, 1977. Travel-size packets labeled Farrah. $10.00 – $15.00.

FAN CLUB KIT, Charlie's Angels, 1970s. Featuring Kelly, Kris, and Sabrina. $75.00 – $100.00.

FAN CLUB KIT, Jaclyn Smith, 1970s. $25.00 – $35.00.

FARRAH'S TRAVEL TRUNK, Mego, 1977. Photo of Farrah on box. For 12" doll. $50.00 – $75.00.

FASHION DRESS-UP SET, HG Toys, 1970s. Includes play watch, shoes, purse, and sunglasses. Window box has photo of Kelly, Kris, and Sabrina. $75.00 – $100.00.

IRON-ONS, 1970s. Several different. $8.00 – $12.00 each.

JEWELRY, The Fawcett, Gadwar, 1970s. Gold-plated faucet with a drip. $50.00 – $75.00.

JIGSAW PUZZLE, Kelly, Stafford Pemberton, 1970s. European. $20.00 – $25.00.

KEYCHAIN, Farrah, 1970s. Color photo of Farrah. $15.00 – $20.00.

MAGIC SLATE, Whitman, 1977. Featuring illustration of Kelly, Kris, and Sabrina. $35.00 – $45.00.

MEMO PADS, Farrah, 1970s. Three different styles. Same photos as notebooks. $10.00 – $15.00 each.

MIRROR, Jill, Sabrina and Kelly 1970s. Vertical black silkscreen on framed mirror. $50.00 – $75.00.

MIRROR, Farrah, 1970s. Black silkscreen on small, framed mirror. $20.00 – $25.00.

PAINT BY NUMBERS DELUXE SET, Hasbro, 1978. Set of three pictures with nine acrylic paints. Box features illustration of Kelly, Kris, and Sabrina. $35.00 – $45.00.

PAPER DOLL BOOKLETS, Sabrina, Kris, and Kelly, Stafford Pemberton, 1970s. European. $25.00 – $30.00 each.

PENCIL CASE, 1970s. $25.00 – $30.00.

PINBALL MACHINE, D. Gottlieb & Co., 1977. Arcade machine with illustrations of Kelly, Kris, and Sabrina. $800.00 – $1,000.00.

PLAY MONEY, Farrah, 1970s. Photo of Farrah in center of different denominations. $10.00 – $15.00 each.

PLAY SET, Toy Factory, 1977. Includes cardboard punchout characters, vehicles, helicopter, and buildings. Box features photo of Jill, Kelly, and Sabrina. $40.00 – $50.00.

POCKETBOOK RADIO, Illco Toys, 1970s. AM radio with microphone, earplug, and vinyl carrying case. Box features photo of Jill, Kelly, and Sabrina. $50.00 – $75.00.

POSTER ART KIT, Board King, 1977. Features Jill, Kelly, and Sabrina. Contains three posters and six markers. $25.00 – $35.00.

POSTER PEN SET, Farrah, Craft House, 1970s. Includes poster on back. $35.00 – $45.00.

RAINY DAY SET, Travel Toy, 1977. Set includes vinyl hat, umbrella, and photo cover rain tote. Box features photo of Kelly, Kris, and Sabrina. $75.00 – $100.00.

RECORD PLAYER, 1970s. $50.00 – $75.00.

RECORD/45, "Charlie's Angels Theme"/"Starsky & Hutch Theme," United Artists, 1976. Original theme from the television show. Instrumentals by The Ventures. $8.00 – $12.00.

RECORDS/LP's, Cheryl Ladd, Capitol, 1970 – 1980s. "Take a Chance," "Greatest Hits," "Cheryl Ladd," and "Dance Forever." Import records from Japan. $25.00 – $30.00 each.

RUGS, Farrah, Zodiac, 1977. Three different styles. $30.00 – $40.00 each.

SHEET MUSIC, Farrah, Burt Productions, Inc. 1970s. $25.00 – $35.00.

THREE-RING BINDERS, Stuart Hall, 1978 – 1981. Different styles. $20.00 – $25.00 each.

TRAVELER'S SET, Fleetwood, 1977. Vinyl bags with logo on card. $15.00 – $20.00.

T-SHIRTS, 1970s. Several different variations with Cheryl, Farrah, Jaclyn, and Kate. $15.00 – $20.00 each.

WALKIE TALKIES, LJN Toys, 1970s. Pair in box. $100.00 – $125.00.

WRIST RADIO, Illco Toys, 1970s. Boxed radio featuring photo of Jill, Kelly, and Sabrina. $75.00 – $100.00.

WRISTWATCH, Farrah, 1970s. $100.00 – $125.00.

CHiPs

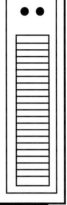

September 15, 1977 – July 18, 1983
135 Episodes
Peak Position: #18 in the 1979 – 1980 season.

Cast

Erik Estrada.............Officer Francis "Ponch" Poncherello
Larry Wilcox..Officer Jon Baker
Robert Pine....................................Sergeant Joe Getraer
Randi Oakes ....Officer Bonnie Clark
Paul Linke..................................Officer Arthur Grossman

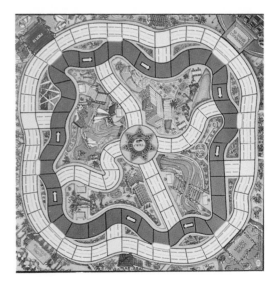

Above and right: BOARD GAME, Ideal, 1981.
$15.00 – $20.00

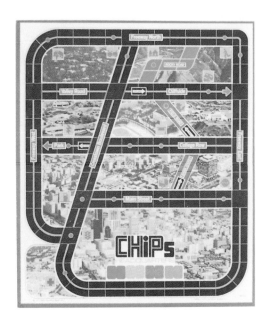

Above and right: BOARD GAME, Milton Bradley, 1977.
$15.00 – $20.00.

Left: BRITISH ANNUALS, World, 1980 – 1983. $15.00 – $20.00 each.

Right: COLORFORMS, Colorforms, 1981. $10.00 – $15.00.

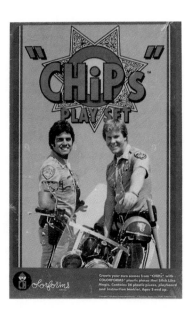

COLORING AND ACTIVITY BOOKS, Waldman, 1983. Four different. #402-3 not pictured. $5.00 – $8.00 each.

CHiPs 73

DIE-CAST MOTORCYCLE, Imperial, 1980. Metal motorcycle with CHiPs logo. $15.00 – $20.00.

EMERGENCY MEDICAL KIT, Empire, 1980. $20.00 – $25.00.

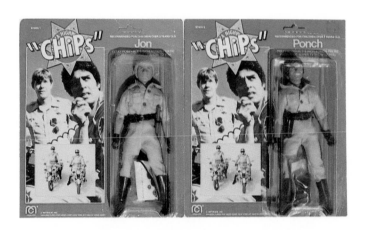

Above and right: DOLLS, Jon, Ponch, and Sarge, Mego, 1980. $20.00 – $25.00 each.

FREE-WHEELING MOTORCYCLE, Mego, 1980. For 8" dolls. $20.00 – $25.00.

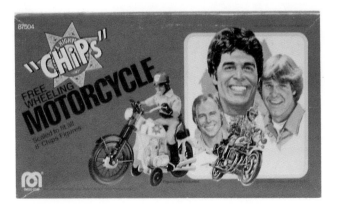

TV Memorabilia

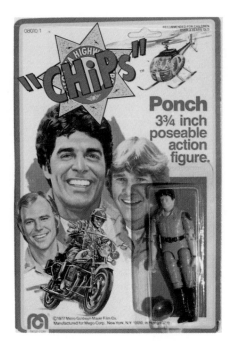

FIGURES, Ponch, Jon, Sarge, Jimmy Squeaks, and Wheels Willie, Mego, 1977. Ponch pictured. $10.00 – $15.00 each.

JIGSAW PUZZLES, HG Toys, 1977. Several different. #483-01 pictured. $8.00 – $10.00 each.

HALLOWEEN COSTUME, CHiPs, Ben Cooper, 1978. $20.00 – $25.00.

LUNCHBOX, Thermos, 1977. Plastic box with plastic thermos. $25.00 – $30.00 box. $8.00 – $12.00 thermos.

MODEL KIT, Helicopter, Revell, 1980. Snap together model kit, 1/32 scale. $15.00 – $20.00.

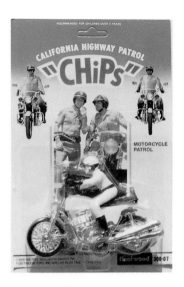

MOTORCYCLE PATROL, Fleetwood, 1978. $8.00 – $12.00.

MODEL KIT, Kawasaki, Revell, 1980. $15.00 – $20.00.

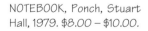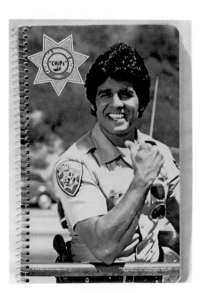

NOTEBOOK, Ponch, Stuart Hall, 1979. $8.00 – $10.00.

POLICE ACCESSORIES SET, Fleetwood, 1978. $10.00 – $15.00.

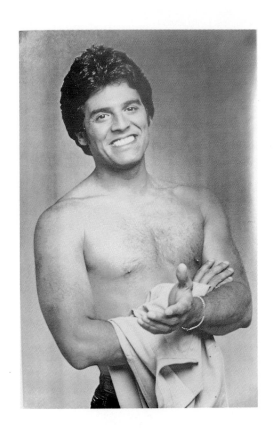

Above and right: POSTERS, Erik Estrada, 1970s.
$10.00 – $15.00 each.

RECORD/45, Theme/"California Hustle,"
Windsong Records, 1979. Instrumentals
by Corniche. $10.00 – $15.00.

TARGET SET, Placo, 1981. $35.00 – $45.00.

VIEW-MASTER #L14, GAF, 1980. $10.00 – $15.00.

TRADING CARDS, Donruss, 1979. 60 numbered and 6 unnumbered stickers in set with puzzle backs.

$25.00 – $30.00 set. $.50 – $.75 single stickers.
$3.00 – $5.00 wrapper. $10.00 – $15.00 display box.

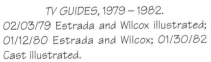

WIND N' WATCH SPEED-STER, Buddy L, 1981.
$15.00 – $20.00.

WALLET, Imperial, 1981.
$8.00 – $12.00.

TV GUIDES, 1979 – 1982.
02/03/79 Estrada and Wilcox illustrated;
01/12/80 Estrada and Wilcox; 01/30/82
Cast illustrated.
$5.00 – $8.00 each.

Other items not pictured:

BICYCLE SIREN, 1970s. $15.00 – $20.00.

BIG WHEEL, 1970s. In box. $50.00 – $75.00.

CAMERA, 1970s. 110 camera on card. $15.00 – $20.00.

DIE-CAST HELICOPTER, Imperial, 1980. Metal helicopter on card. $15.00 – $20.00.

GUN HOLSTER AND BADGE SET, 1981. On illustrated card. $15.00 – $20.00.

HELICOPTER, Empire, 1980. 2' play helicopter in box. $25.00 – $35.00.

HIGHWAY PATROL LAUNCHER AND MOTORCYCLE, Mego, 1981. For 8" dolls. $25.00 – $35.00.

MODEL KIT, Ponch's Firebird, Revell, 1980. With t-shirt iron-on. $20.00 – $25.00.

MODEL KIT, Z-28 Chase Car, Revell, 1981. With t-shirt iron-on. $20.00 – $25.00.

MOTORCYCLE AND BADGE SET, 1977. Set on card. $10.00 – $15.00.

MOTORCYCLE HELMET SET, 1970s. Window box includes guns, hand-cuffs, and walkie-talkies. $50.00 – $75.00.

PATROL 4-WHEELER, Imperial 1980s. Vehicle on card. $8.00 – $12.00.

PATROL VAN, Imperial, 1980s. Vehicle on card. $8.00 – $12.00.

POLICE SET, 1970s. Police accessories in a photo window box. $25.00 – $30.00.

PUFFY STICKERS, Imperial, 1970s. $8.00 – $12.00 each.

RESCUE BRONCO WITH LAUNCHER, Fleetwood, 1979. Wind-up motorcycle wristband. $20.00 – $25.00.

RESCUE HELICOPTER, Fleetwood, 1979. With operating wench and rescue lifter on photo card. $20.00 – $25.00.

SLEEPING BAG, 1977. $25.00 – $35.00.

SLOT CAR RACING SET, Ideal, 1980s. Motorcycle and van in illustrated box. $35.00 – $45.00.

SUNGLASSES, Fleetwood, 1977. On card. $10.00 – $15.00.

VAN, Empire, 1980. Play van in box for 8" dolls. $35.00 – $45.00.

DONNY AND MARIE

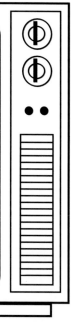

January 23, 1976 – January 19, 1979
57 Episodes
Peak Position: Not in the top 25.

Cast
Donny Osmond
Marie Osmond
Jimmy Osmond

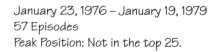

ADDRESS BOOK, Continental Plastics Corp., 1977.
$8.00 – $12.00.

Right top and bottom:
BOARD GAME, Mattel, 1977.
$25.00 – $30.00.

BOOKS, *Disco Dancing with Donny and Marie* and *Close Dancing with Donny and Marie*, Osmond Publishing Co., 1979. $3.00 – $5.00 each.

BUTTONS, Pinning Co., 1976. 3" in diameter. Different styles. $3.00 – $5.00 each.

COLORFORMS DRESS-UP SET, Colorforms, 1977. $20.00 – $25.00.

COUNTRY ROCK AND RHYTHM SET, Gordy, 1976. $10.00 – $15.00.

COLORING BOOK #1641, Whitman, 1977. Paper dolls on back with clothes to color inside. $10.00 – $15.00.

DIARY, Continental Plastics, 1977. $8.00 – $12.00.

DOLL CASE, Mattel, 1978. $15.00 – $20.00.

DOLL, Jimmy, Mattel, 1978. Canadian release pictured. $50.00— $75.00.

DOLLS, Donny and Marie, Mattel, 1976. Also sold as a gift set in one box.
   $20.00 – $25.00 each. $40.00 – $60.00 gift set.

DOLL OUTFITS, Mattel, 1977. Several styles for Donny and Marie 12" dolls. Came in deluxe boxes and on cards. Deluxe Donny Glimmer O' Gold pictured. $10.00 – $15.00 each.

DOLL, Marie, Mattel, 1976. 30" modeling doll. In photo cover box with dress patterns inside. $60.00 – $80.00.

FRAME TRAY PUZZLES #B4542-1 and #B4542-2, Whitman, 1977. $8.00 – $10.00 each.

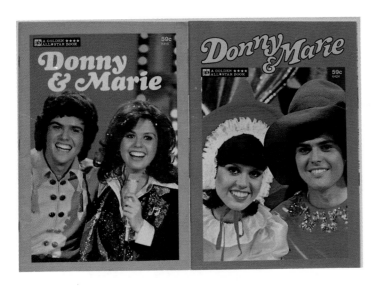

GOLDEN ALL-STAR BOOKS, Golden Press, 1977. $5.00 – $8.00 each.

GUITAR, Lapin, 1977.
$30.00 – $40.00.

HALLOWEEN COSTUME, Donny, Collegeville,
1977. $15.00 – $20.00.

HALLOWEEN COSTUME, Marie, Collegeville, 1977. $15.00 – $20.00.

HALLOWEEN COSTUME, Jimmy, Collegeville, 1977.
$15.00 – $20.00.

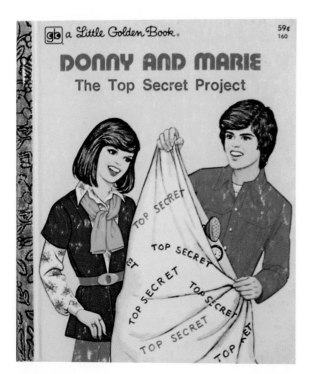

LITTLE GOLDEN BOOK, *Top Secret Project*,
Golden Press, 1977. $5.00 – $8.00.

LUNCH BOX, Aladdin, 1976. Vinyl box and plastic thermos.
$50.00 – $75.00 box. $10.00 – $15.00 thermos.

LUNCH BOX, Aladdin, 1977. Vinyl box and plastic thermos.
$50.00 – $75.00 box. $10.00 – $15.00 thermos.

MARIE'S STYLING HEAD, Mattel, 1978. $35.00 – $45.00.

MARIE'S MAKE UP SET, Gordy, 1976.
$10.00 – $15.00.

MICROPHONE AND SONG SHEETS,
Gordy, 1976. $10.00 – $15.00.

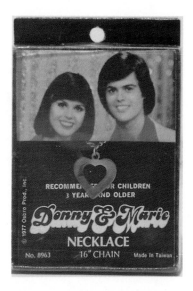

NECKLACE, *Osbro*, 1977.
$10.00 – $15.00.

PAPER DOLL BOOKLET #1991, Whitman, 1977.
$10.00 – $15.00.

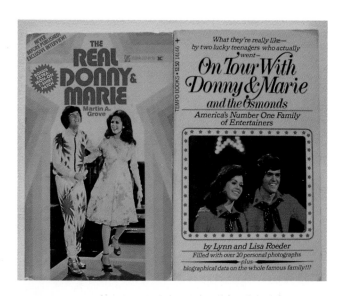

PAPERBACK BOOKS, *The Real Donny and Marie*, Zebra Books,
1977 and *On Tour With Donny and Marie*, Tempo Books, 1977.
The Real Donny and Marie includes a T-shirt iron-on inside.
$3.00 – $5.00 each.

PORTABLE RECORD PLAYERS, *Peerless Vidtronic
Corp.*, 1977. Two different styles to match record
carrying cases. Yellow version not pictured.
$30.00 – $40.00 each.

PORTABLE RECORD PLAYER AND AM RADIO, L.J.N. Toys, 1977. Comes with microphone to sing along. $30.00 – $40.00.

POSTER, Donny and Marie Collage, Dargis Associates Inc., 1976. $10.00 – $15.00.

POSTER PEN SET, Craft House, 1977. Color poster on back. $15.00 – $20.00.

RECORDS/LP's, "Donny and Marie" and "New Season," Polydor, 1976. These are the only albums dedicated to the television show. $5.00 – $8.00 each.

RECORD CARRYING CASES, Peerless Vidtronic Corp., 1977. Red version for LP's and 45's. $20.00 – $25.00 each.

RECORD CARRYING CASES, Peerless Vidtronic Corp., 1977. Yellow version for LP's and 45's. $20.00 – $25.00 each.

STICKER BOOK, Whitman, 1977. $10.00 – $15.00.

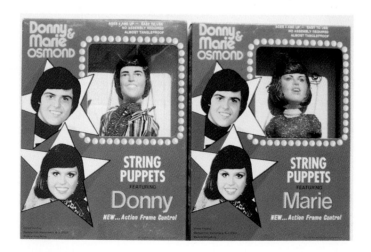

STRING PUPPETS, Donny and Marie, Madison, 1978. Also sold as a gift set in one box.
$25.00 – $30.00 each. $50.00 – $60.00 gift set.

TELEVISION STAGE SET, Mattel, 1978. Playset for 12" dolls. Includes flexible record. $40.00-$60.00.

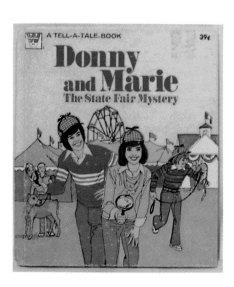

TELL-A-TALE BOOK, *The State Fair Mystery*, Whitman, 1977. $3.00 – $5.00.

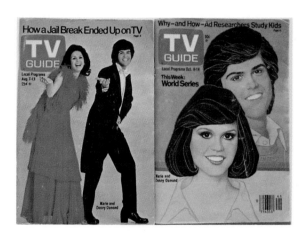

TV GUIDES, 1976 – 1977.
08/07/76, Donny and Marie
10/08/77, Donny and Marie illustrated.
$3.00 – $5.00 each.

VAN, Lapin, 1978. $30.00 – $40.00.

WALLET AND MONEY SET, Gordy, 1976. $10.00 – $15.00.

Other items not pictured:

BRUNCH BAG, Aladdin, 1976. Vinyl bag with plastic thermos. Marie with long hair. $50.00 – $75.00 bag; $10.00 – $15.00 thermos.

BRUNCH BAG, Aladdin, 1977. Vinyl bag with plastic thermos. Marie with short hair. $50.00 – $75.00 bag; $10.00 – $15.00 thermos.

BUTTONS, 1970s. 2⅛" diameter. 16 different styles. $3.00 – $5.00 each.

CANDLES, 1970s. 10" figures holding microphones and standing on platforms. Each has their name in bold letters. $25.00 – $30.00 each.

CHARM BRACELETS, 1970s. 8 different charms with portraits and signatures. $10.00 – $15.00 each.

COLOR YOUR OWN MUGS, Craft House, 1977. $15.00 – $20.00.

COUNTRY & ROCK BAND, Gordy, 1976. Three plastic instruments on photo card. $10.00 – $15.00.

DONNY'S PURPLE SOCKS, 1970s. Color photo of Donny on each sock. $15.00 – $20.00.

DRUM SET, 1977. Play drum set in box. $50.00 – $75.00.

IRON-ONS, 1970s, Several different. $8.00 – $12.00 each.

KEYCHAIN, 1970s. Purple sock with Donny's signature on back. $8.00 – $12.00.

KEYS AND WATCH, Gordy, 1976. On card with photo. $10.00 – $15.00.

MAGIC SET, Gordy, 1976. Donny and Marie's photo featured on card. $10.00 – $15.00.

MARIE'S BEAUTY CASE, Osbro, 1977. 11" x 11" x 3" purple vinyl case with color photo of Marie. $20.00 – $25.00.

MARIE'S HAIR DRYER SET, Gordy, 1976. Marie's photo featured on card. $10.00 – $15.00.

MARIE'S JEWELRY, Gordy, 1976. Marie's photo featured on card. $10.00 – $15.00.

MARIE'S VANITY SET, Gordy, 1976. Marie's photo featured on box. $15.00 – $20.00.

MESSAGE BOARD, 1970s. Circle photo of Donny and Marie in upper left corner with pen attached. $10.00 – $15.00.

NECKLACE, 1970s. Roses on a heart with Marie's signature on back. $10.00 – $15.00.

POCKET AM RADIO, L.J.N. Toys, 1977. 3" x 5" blue radio with silver trim, color photo, and carrying strap. $20.00 – $25.00.

PORTABLE SING ALONG AM RADIO, L.J.N. Toys, 1977. White plastic with photo and microphone on side. $25.00 – $35.00.

READING PROGRAM, 1978. Includes tape of hits. $10.00 – $20.00.

SHEET MUSIC, Osmusic, 1977. Several different, including theme "May Tomorrow Be A Perfect Day." $5.00 – $8.00 each.

TOOTHBRUSH, Pamco, 1977. Battery-operated. $25.00 – $30.00.

TRAVEL SETS, Donny and Marie, 1970s. Comb and brush in photo box. $15.00 – $20.00.

WIRELESS MICROPHONE, L.J.N. Toys, 1977. Donny and Marie's photo featured on window box. $25.00 – $35.00.

EIGHT IS ENOUGH

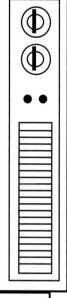

March 15, 1977 – August 29, 1981
112 Episodes
Peak Position: #11 in the 1978 – 1979 season.

Cast

Dick Van Patten	Tom Bradford
Diana Hyland	Joan Bradford
Betty Buckley	Sandra "Abby" Bradford
Grant Goodeve	David
Lani O'Grady	Mary
Laurie Walters	Joanie
Susan Richardson	Susan
Dianne Kay	Nancy
Willie Aames	Tommy
Connie Needham	Elizabeth
Adam Rich	Nicholas

JIGSAW PUZZLE, APC, 1978. $10.00 – $15.00.

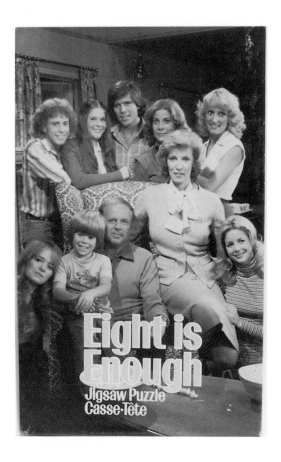

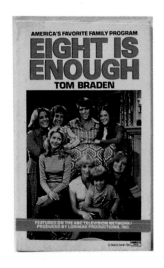

PAPERBACK BOOK, Fawcett
Crest, 1975. $5.00 – $8.00.

TV GUIDE.
12/16/78. $5.00 – $8.00.

VIEW-MASTER #K76, GAF, 1980. $10.00 – $15.00.

Other items not pictured:

KITE FUN BOOK, Western Publishing, 1979. 5" x 7" comic book distributed by the electric company with comics, activities, and
instructions for safe kite flying. $10.00 – $15.00.

POSTER, Collage, 1970s. $15.00 – $20.00.

FAMILY

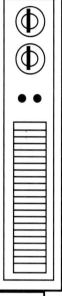

March 9, 1976 – June 25, 1980
94 Episodes
Peak Position: Not in the top 25.

Cast

James Broderick......................................Douglas Lawrence
Sada Thompson...Kate Lawrence
Meredith Baxter Birney...........................Nancy Maitland
Gary Frank...Willie
Kristy McNichol...Buddy
Quinn Cummings..Annie

PAPERBACK BOOKS #1 – 3, Ballantine, 1976 – 1977.
$3.00 – $5.00 each.

DOLL, Kristy McNichol as Buddy, Mattel, 1978.
$25.00 – $30.00.

DOLL, Kristy McNichol, Mego, 1978.
$25.00 – $30.00.

TV GUIDES, 1978 – 1980.
01/21/78 Cast (not pictured)
03/15/80 Cast.
$3.00 – $5.00 each.

FAMILY AFFAIR

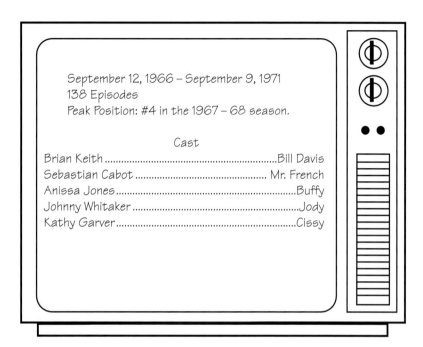

September 12, 1966 – September 9, 1971
138 Episodes
Peak Position: #4 in the 1967 – 68 season.

Cast

Brian Keith ....Bill Davis
Sebastian Cabot .... Mr. French
Anissa Jones..Buffy
Johnny Whitaker ....Jody
Kathy Garver...Cissy

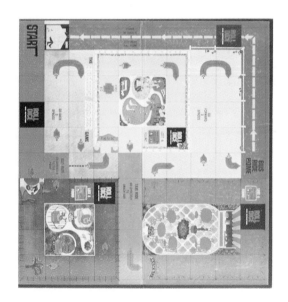

Above and right: BOARD GAME, Remco, 1968. $50.00 – $75.00.

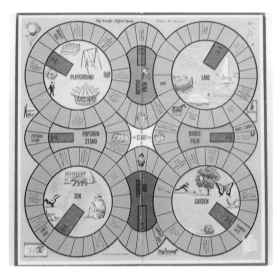

Above and right: BOARD GAME, Where's Mrs. Beasley?, Whitman, 1971. $30.00 – $40.00.

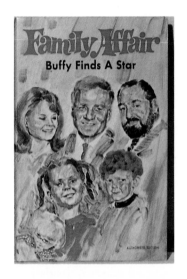

Left: BOOK, *Buffy Finds a Star*, Whitman, 1970. $8.00 – $10.00.

Right: BUFFY MAKE-UP AND HAIRSTYLING SET, Amsco, 1971. $40.00 – $50.00.

Left: COLORING BOOK #1408, Whitman, 1969. Color by number. $15.00 – $20.00.

Right: CARTOON KIT, Colorforms, 1970. $25.00 – $35.00.

COLORING BOOK #1414, Whitman, 1969. Trace and color. $15.00 – $20.00.

COLORING BOOK #1640, Whitman, 1968. $15.00 – $20.00.

COLORING BOOK #1640, Whitman, 1968. $15.00 – $20.00.

COLORING BOOK #1364, Mrs. Beasley, Whitman, 1972. Color and read. $15.00 – $20.00.

Right: COLORING BOOK #1110, Mrs. Beasley, Whitman, 1970. $15.00 – $20.00.

COLORING BOOK #1033, Mrs. Beasley, Whitman, 1970. $15.00 – $20.00.

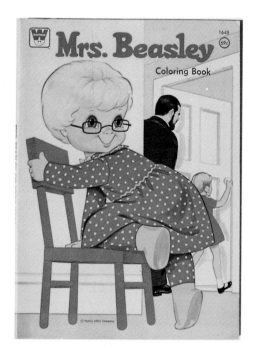

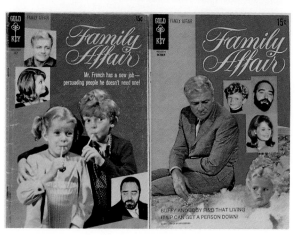

COLORING BOOK #1648, Mrs. Beasley, Whitman, 1975. $15.00 – $20.00.

Right center and bottom: COMIC BOOKS #1 – 4, Gold Key, 1969 – 1970. #1 includes Buffy pull-out poster. $20.00 – $25.00 #1. $10.00 – $15.00 #2 – 4.

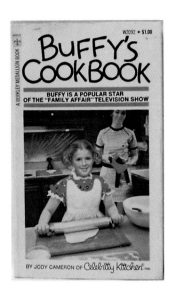

COOKBOOK, *Buffy's Cookbook,*
Berkley, 1971. $8.00 – $12.00.

DOLLS, Buffy and Mrs. Beasley,
Mattel, 1967. 6" Buffy with 3" Mrs.
Beasley. Mrs. Beasley not pictured.
$45.00 – $65.00 loose set.
$100.00 – $125.00 boxed set.

DOLLS, Buffy and Mrs. Beasley, Mattel, 1967. 10"
talking Buffy with 4" Mrs. Beasley.
$65.00 – $85.00 loose set.
$125.00 – $175.00 boxed set.

FRAME TRAY PUZZLE #4558, Whitman, 1971.
$25.00 – $35.00.

JIGSAW PUZZLE #4426, Whitman, 1970.
$25.00 – $30.00.

JIGSAW PUZZLE #4609, Whitman, 1970.
$25.00 – $30.00.

PAPER DOLL BOOKLET, Buffy, Whitman, 1968. $25.00 – $30.00.

LUNCH BOX, K.S.T., 1969. Metal box with metal thermos.
$40.00 – $50.00 box. $20.00 – $25.00 thermos.

PAPER DOLL BOOKLET, Buffy, Whitman, 1969.
$25.00 – $30.00.

PAPER DOLL BOX #4764,
Buffy and Jody, Whitman,
1970. $25.00 – $35.00.

PAPER DOLL BOOKLET #1973, Mrs.
Beasley, Whitman, 1970. $20.00 – $25.00.

PAPER DOLL BOOKLET #1993, Mrs. Beasley, Whitman,
1972. $15.00 – $20.00.

PAPER DOLL BOX
#4767, Whitman, 1970.
$25.00 – $35.00.

PAPER DOLL BOX #4339/
7420, Mrs. Beasley, Whitman,
1974. $20.00 – $25.00.

RAG DOLLS, Mrs. Beasley, Mattel, 1968. 10" doll in red or blue dress.
$8.00 – $12.00 each.

RAG DOLL, Mrs. Beasley, Mattel, 1973. 14" doll. $30.00 – $40.00.

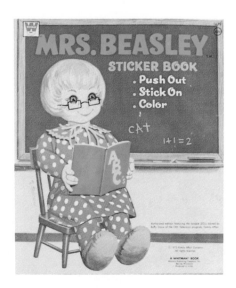

STICKER BOOK #1679, Mrs. Beasley, Whitman, 1972. $25.00 – $35.00.

TELL-A-TALE BOOK, Buffy and the New Girl, Whitman, 1969. $8.00 – $12.00.

RAG DOLL, Mrs. Beasley, Mattel, 1967. 21" talking doll. Original boxed doll includes dress and glasses.
$50.00 – $75.00 loose.
$150.00 – $200.00 boxed.

TV GUIDES, 1967 – 1969.
04/22/67 Jones, Cabot, and Keith;
12/16/67 Sebastian Cabot (not pictured); 09/07/68 Cast; 05/31/69
Jones, Cabot, and Whitaker.
$8.00 – $12.00 each.

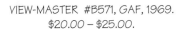

VIEW-MASTER #B571, GAF, 1969.
$20.00 – $25.00.

WIG CASES, Amsco, 1969 – 1971. Pink case, 1969 and yellow case, 1970. Yellow case,
1971, not pictured. $20.00 – $25.00 each.

Other items not pictured:

ALARM CLOCK, 1960s. Illustration of Buffy and Jody. $75.00 – $100.00.

BUFFY BUTTONS, 1960s. Several different styles on card. Made for clothing line.
$10.00 – $15.00 each.

BUFFY DRESS, Cinderella, 1960s. From clothing line with tag featuring Buffy. $100.00 – $150.00.

COLORING BOOK #1640, Buffy and Jody, Whitman, 1969. Illustration of Jody and Buffy running in
park. $15.00 – $20.00.

HALLOWEEN COSTUME, Buffy, Ben Cooper, 1970. $50.00 – $75.00.

STICKER BOOK #2170, Mrs. Beasley, Whitman, 1975. $25.00 – $35.00.

FANTASY ISLAND

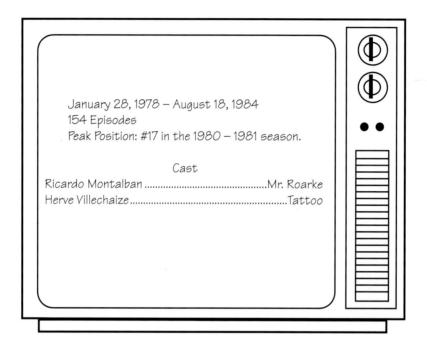

January 28, 1978 – August 18, 1984
154 Episodes
Peak Position: #17 in the 1980 – 1981 season.

Cast

Ricardo Montalban ....Mr. Roarke
Herve Villechaize...Tattoo

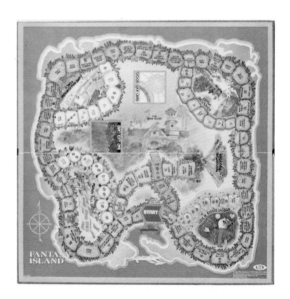

Above and right: BOARD GAME, Ideal, 1978. $20.00 – $25.00.

HALLOWEEN COSTUME, Tattoo, Ben Cooper, 1978.
$25.00 – $30.00.

JIGSAW PUZZLE, HG Toys, 1977. $10.00 – $15.00.

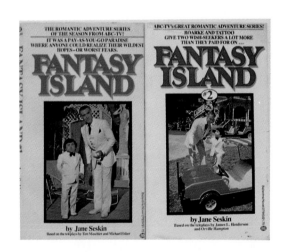

PAPERBACK BOOKS #1 – 2, Ballantine Books, 1978 – 1979.
$5.00 – $8.00 each.

Left: PAPERBACK BOOK, Fantasy Island, Weekly Reader, 1981.
$5.00 – $8.00.

Right: TV GUIDES, 1978 – 1980. 07/01/78 Cast illustrated; 03/24/79 Montalban illustrated; 03/01/80 Cast illustrated (not pictured).
$5.00 – $8.00 each.

FLIPPER

September 19, 1964 – May 14, 1967
88 Episodes
Peak Position: #25 in the 1964 – 1965 season.

Cast
Brian Kelly...Porter Ricks
Luke Halpin ....Sandy
Tommy Norden...Bud

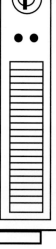

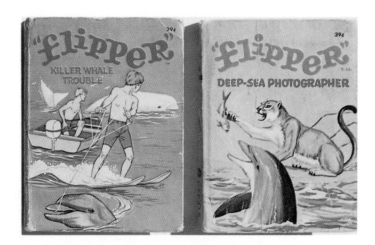

BIG LITTLE BOOKS, *Killer Whale Trouble* and *Deep-Sea Photographer*,
Whitman, 1967. $8.00 – $10.00 each.

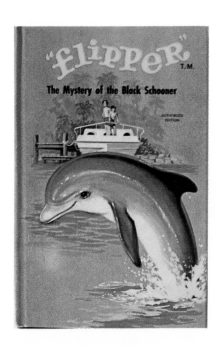

BOOK, *The Mystery of the Black Schooner*,
Whitman, 1966. $5.00 – $8.00.

Above and right: BOARD GAME, Flipper Flips, Mattel, 1965.
$50.00 – $75.00.

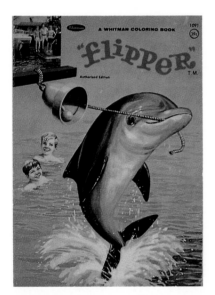

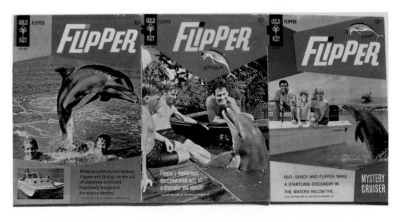

COMIC BOOKS #1 – 3, Gold Key, 1966 – 1967. $10.00 – $15.00 each.

COLORING BOOK #1091, Whitman, 1966.
$15.00 – $20.00.

FRAME TRAY PUZZLE #4526, Whitman, 1965. $15.00 – $20.00.

FRAME TRAY PUZZLE #4546, Whitman, 1966.
$15.00 – $20.00.

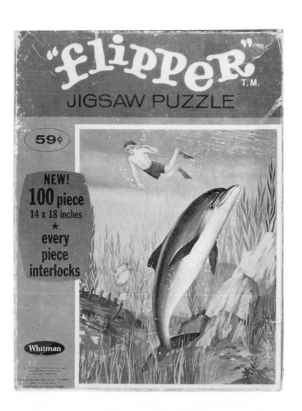

JIGSAW PUZZLES, Whitman, 1965 – 1968. Several different
boxed versions. 1967 puzzle pictured. $20.00 – $25.00 each.

JIGSAW PUZZLE, Whitman, 1967. 99-piece puzzle in a box that resembles A Big Little Book.
$10.00 – $15.00.

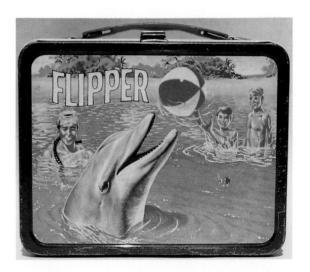

LUNCH BOX , K.S.T., 1966. Metal box with metal thermos.
$80.00 – $100.00 box. $30.00 – $40.00 thermos.

PLASTIC STICK-ONS, Standard Toykraft, 1965.
$35.00 – $45.00.

SONG BOOK, Leo Feist, Inc., 1965.
$10.00 – $15.00.

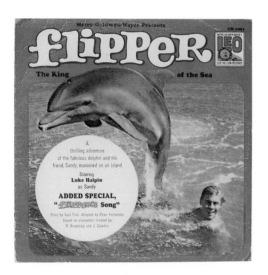

Left: RECORD/LP, "Flipper, The King of the Sea," MGM, 1960s. Includes adventure stories and "Flipper's Song." $15.00 – $20.00.

Right: TALKING VIEW-MASTER #AVB45, GAF, 1966. $25.00 – $30.00.

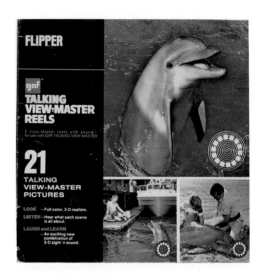

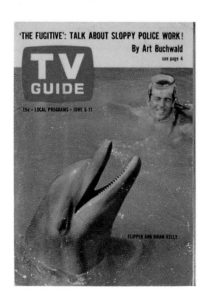

Left: *TV GUIDES*, 1965 – 1966. 06/05/65 Flipper and Kelly; 07/09/66 Flipper and Kelly (not pictured).
$8.00 – $10.00 each.

Right: VIEW-MASTER #B485, Sawyer, 1966. $15.00 – $20.00.

Other items not pictured:

ACTIVITY BOX, Whitman, 1966. 16 pictures to complete with crayons and paste. $40.00 – $50.00.

BANK, 1960s. 17½" plastic figural. $50.00 – $75.00.

BATHTUB PUMP, Louis A. Boettiger, 1968. On illustrated card. $50.00 – $75.00.

BATTERY-OPERATED SPOUTING DOLPHIN, Bandai, 1968. $75.00 – $100.00.

CIGAR BANDS, 1970s. European set of 24. Bands with photos of each character. $40.00 – $50.00.

COLOR BY NUMBER SET, Hasbro, 1966. $40.00 – $50.00.

COLORING BOOK #1122, Whitman, 1966. $15.00 – $20.00.

COLORING BOOK #1851, Watkins-Strathmore, 1960s. $15.00 – $20.00.

COLORING BOOK #2843, Lowe, 1960s. $15.00 – $20.00.

COLORING BOOK #2845, Lowe, 1960s. Flipper and Sandy on cover. $15.00 – $20.00.

FLIPPER'S MAGIC FISH, Topps, 1960s. 10 different fish in set. Came in gumless paper wrappers. $150.00 – $200.00 set; $15.00 – $20.00 single fish; $30.00 – $40.00 wrapper.

FRAME TRAY PUZZLES, Whitman, 1966. Set of 4 in a box. $60.00 – $80.00.

HALLOWEEN COSTUME, Flipper, Collegeville, 1964. $60.00 – $80.00.

INFLATABLE TOY, Coleco, 1966. Blow-up punching bag of Flipper. $50.00 – $75.00.

MAGIC SLATE, Lowe, 1960s. Illustration of Sandy on Flipper's back. $30.00 – $40.00.

MODEL KIT, Revell, 1965. Flipper jumps out of water with Sandy holding a fish. $50.00 – $75.00.

MUSICAL UKULELE, Mattel, 1968. Guitar-like with illustration of Flipper. $75.00 – $100.00.

MUSIC BOX, Mattel, 1966. Metal box with crank. Flipper pops out like a jack-in-the-box. $125.00 – $150.00.

PAINT WITH WATER BOOK #1340, Whitman, 1964. $15.00 – $20.00.

PINBACK BUTTONS, 1964. Different styles, including Bud, Flipper, and Bud and Flipper. $8.00 – $12.00 each.

RECORD/78, "Theme to Flipper"/"Anchors Aweigh," Golden Records, 1960s. Vocals by The Golden Dolphins and The Golden Naval Chorus. $15.00 – $20.00.

RIDING TOY, Irwin, 1965. Figural Flipper with handles for riding. $125.00 – $175.00.

RUB-ONS #2746, Hasbro, 1960s. $30.00 – $40.00.

SQUIRT GUN FIGURAL, 1960s. Water toy on card. $30.00 – $40.00.

STARDUST TOUCH OF VELVET BY NUMBERS, 1960s. $20.00 – $25.00.

STICKER BOOK, Whitman, 1967. $20.00 – $30.00.

STITCH-A-STORY, Hasbro, 1966. $40.00 – $50.00.

TRADING CARDS, Topps, 1966. Test set of 30. No wrapper or box exist. Photo cards with puzzle backs. $1,500.00 – $1,700.00 set; $40.00 – $50.00 single cards.

TRU-VUE SET, 1964. Rectangular 3-D viewer cards. $20.00 – $30.00.

VIEW-MASTER, Sawyer, 1966. Triangular version. $15.00 – $20.00.

WATCH, 1960s. $150.00 – $175.00.

THE FLYING NUN

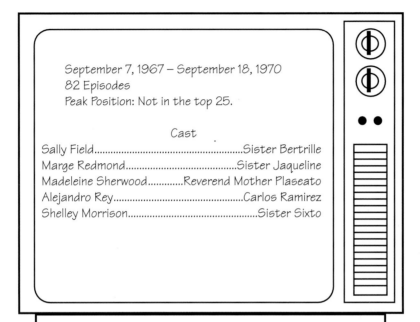

September 7, 1967 – September 18, 1970
82 Episodes
Peak Position: Not in the top 25.

Cast
Sally Field...Sister Bertrille
Marge Redmond.......................................Sister Jaqueline
Madeleine Sherwood.............Reverend Mother Plaseato
Alejandro Rey...Carlos Ramirez
Shelley Morrison.....................................Sister Sixto

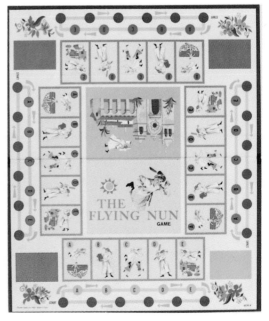

Above and right: BOARD GAME, Milton Bradley, 1968. $30.00 – $40.00.

CHALK BOARD, Screen Gems, 1967. $50.00 – $75.00.

COLORING BOOK #4572, Saalfield, 1968.
$25.00 – $35.00.

Left: DOLL, Sister Bertrille, Hasbro,
1960s. 4" doll. $50.00 – $75.00.

Right: LUNCH BOX, Aladdin, 1968.
Metal box with metal thermos.
$75.00 – $100.00 box.
$25.00 – $30.00 thermos.

COMIC BOOKS #1 – 4, Dell, 1967. $10.00 – $20.00 each.

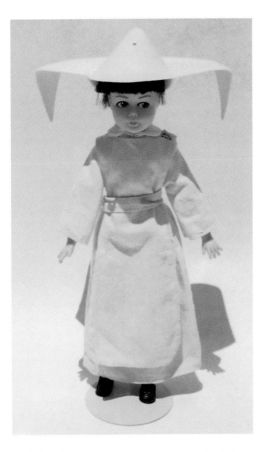

DOLL, Sister Bertrille, Hasbro, 1967. 11" doll.
$50.00 – 75.00 loose. $125.00 – $150.00 boxed.

PAPER DOLL BOOKLET #1317, Saalfield, 1969.
$35.00 – $45.00.

PAPER DOLL BOX #6069, Saalfield, 1969.
$45.00 – $60.00.

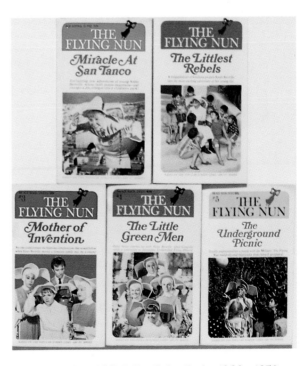

PAPERBACK BOOKS #1 – 5, Ace Books, 1968 – 1970.
$8.00 – $10.00 each.

RECORD/LP, "Sally Field, Star of The Flying Nun," Colgems, 1967. Vocals by Sally Field. $25.00 – $35.00.

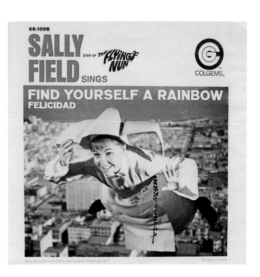

RECORD/45, "Felicidad"/"Find Yourself a Rainbow,"
Colgems, 1967. Vocals by Sally Field.
$15.00 – $20.00.

SHEET MUSIC, "Felicidad," Columbia, 1967.
$15.00 – $20.00.

TRADING CARDS, Donruss, 1968. 66 cards in set with puzzle backs.
$150.00 – $200.00 set. $3.00 – $4.00 single cards.
$10.00 – $15.00 wrapper. $40.00 – $50.00 display box.

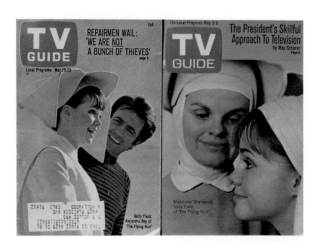

TV GUIDES, 1968 – 1969.
09/30/67 Field (not pictured);
03/16/68 Field and Rey;
05/03/69 Field and Sherwood.
$10.00 – $15.00 each.

VIEW-MASTER #B495, GAF, 1967.
$25.00 – $35.00.

Other items not pictured:

BRUNCH BAG, Aladdin, 1968. Vinyl bag with plastic thermos. $150.00 – $200.00 bag; $30.00 – $40.00 thermos.

COLOR BY NUMBER SET, Hasbro, 1960s. $40.00 – $50.00.

DOLL, Sister Bertrille, 1960s. 14" boxed doll. $150.00 – $200.00.

DOLL, Sister Bertrille, Hasbro, 1960s. 18" boxed doll. $150.00 – $200.00.

FLYING TOY, Rayline, 1970. Water launch toy with photo cover. $30.00 – $40.00.

HALLOWEEN COSTUME, The Flying Nun, 1967. $40.00 – $50.00.

MARBLE MAZE GAME, Hasbro, 1967. Square box with illustration of Sister Bertrille. $40.00 – $50.00.

OIL PAINTING BY NUMBERS SET, Hasbro, 1967. Photo cover box includes 2 scenes, brush, and 10 vials of paint. $50.00 – $60.00.

PAPER DOLL BOOKLET, #5124, Artcraft, 1968. $35.00 – $45.00.

PAPER DOLL BOOKLET #5134, Saalfield, 1968. $35.00 – $45.00.

RECORDS/45's, "Month's of the Year"/"Gonna Build a Mountain" and "You're a Grand Old Flag"/"Golden Days," Colgems, 1967. Without picture sleeves. Vocals by Sally Field. $8.00 – $12.00 each.

SONGBOOK, Columbia, 1967. Photo cover. $25.00 – $30.00.

GIDGET

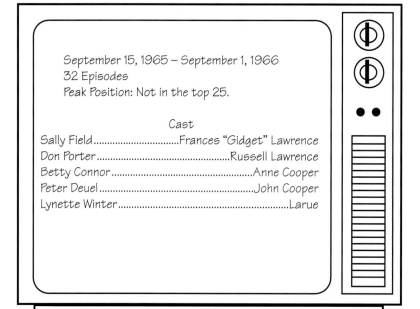

September 15, 1965 – September 1, 1966
32 Episodes
Peak Position: Not in the top 25.

Cast

Sally Field................................Frances "Gidget" Lawrence
Don Porter..Russell Lawrence
Betty Connor..Anne Cooper
Peter Deuel..John Cooper
Lynette Winter..Larue

Above and right: BOARD GAME, Standard Toykraft, 1965.
$50.00 – $75.00.

Above and right: CARD GAME, Fortune Teller Game, Milton Bradley, 1966. $20.00 – $25.00.

PAPER DOLL BOX, Standard Toykraft, 1965. $50.00 – $75.00.

COMIC BOOKS #1 – 2 Dell, 1966. #1 not pictured. $25.00 – $35.00 each.

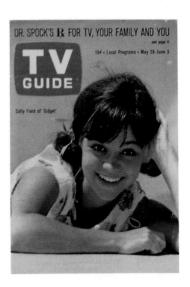

TV GUIDE, 05/28/66. $10.00 – $15.00.

Other items not pictured:

RECORD/45, "(Wait 'til You See) My Gidget"/"Our World," MGM, 1965. Theme from the television show. Vocals by Johnny Tillotson. Without picture sleeve. $5.00 – $8.00.

GILLIGAN'S ISLAND

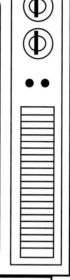

September 26, 1964 – September 3, 1967
98 Episodes
Peak Position: #18 in the 1964 – 1965 season.

Cast

Bob Denver..Gilligan
Alan Hale Jr..................................Jonas "Skipper" Grumby
Jim Backus...Thurston Howell III
Natalie Schafer...Lovey Howell
Tina Louise...Ginger Grant
Russell Johnson ....Professor Roy Hinkley
Dawn Wells......................................Mary Ann Summers

September 7, 1974 – September 4, 1977
24 episodes of The New Adventures of Gilligan
animated cartoon.

BOARD GAME, The New Adventures of Gilligan, Milton Bradley, 1974.
$20.00 – $25.00.

BOOK, Gilligan's Island, Whitman, 1966.
$15.00 – $20.00.

COLORING BOOK #1135, Whitman, 1965. $30.00 – $35.00.

COLORING BOOK, The New Adventures of Gilligan, Kenner, 1975. $25.00 – $30.00.

FIGURES, Gilligan, Skipper, and Mary Ann, Playskool, 1977. Three sold as a separate set. Also came in floating island playset. From cartoon series. $15.00 – $20.00 set.

WRITING TABLE, 1960s. $15.00 – $20.00.

FLOATING ISLAND PLAYSET, Playskool, 1977. From cartoon series. $60.00 – $80.00.

TV GUIDES, 1965 – 1966.
05/08/65 Louise and Denver; 05/11/66 Denver,
Hale, and Louise (not pictured).
$10.00 – $15.00 each.

TRADING CARDS, Topps, 1965. 55 cards in set. Backs of cards have
photos that create a mini-movie when fanned.
    $600.00 – $800.00 set. $10.00 – $15.00 single cards.
    $50.00 – $75.00 wrapper. $250.00 – $300.00 display box.

Other items not pictured:

BOARD GAME, Game Gems, 1965. Cover photo of Mr. Howell, Gilligan, and
the Skipper with illustrated bodies on boat. $200.00 – $250.00.

GOOD TIMES

February 8, 1974 – August 1, 1979
120 Episodes
Peak Position: #7 in the 1974 – 1975 season.

Cast

John Amos ....James Evans
Esther Rolle...Florida Evans
Jimmie Walker.................................James "J.J." Evans, Jr.
BernNadette Stanis...Thelma
Ralph Carter...Michael
Ja'net DuBois...Wilona Woods
Janet Jackson...Penny Gordon
Johnny Brown..Nathan Bookman

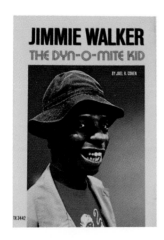

PAPERBACK BOOK, *Jimmie Walker: The Dyn-O-Mite Kid*, Scholastic, 1976. $5.00 – $8.00.

RECORD/LP, "Dyn-O-Mite," Buddah Records, 1975. Spoken comedy by Jimmie Walker. $10.00 – $15.00.

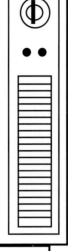

Right: DOLL, J.J., Shindana, 1975. $30.00 – $40.00.

RECORD/LP, "Young and In Love," Mercury, 1976. Vocals by
Ralph Carter. $8.00 – $12.00.

TRADING CARDS, Topps, 1975. 55 cards and 21 stickers in set.
44 cards have puzzle backs and 11 have behind the scenes trivia.
$40.00 – $50.00 set with stickers. $.50 – $.75 single cards.
$.75 – $1.00 single stickers. $3.00 – $5.00 wrapper.
$15.00 – $20.00 display box.

TV GUIDES, 1974.
06/29/74 Rolle and Amos; 12/14/74 Cast.
$5.00 – $8.00 each.

Other items not pictured:

DOLL, Talking J.J., Shindana, 1975. $40.00 – $50.00.

RECORDS/45's Mercury, 1975 – 1976.
"When You're Young and In Love," "Extra, Extra Read All
About It," "Number One In My Heart"/"Headin' Back To
Love Again." Vocals by Ralph Carter. Without picture
sleeves. $3.00 – $5.00 each.

GREEN ACRES

Septembeer 15, 1965 – September 7, 1971
170 Episodes
Peak Position: #6 in the 1966 – 1967 season.

Cast

Eddie Albert... Oliver Douglas
Eva Gabor ....Lisa Douglas
Pat Buttram... Eustace Haney
Tom Lester...Eb Dawson

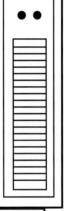

TV GUIDES, 1966 – 1970.
01/08/66 Gabor and Albert;
09/03/66 Gabor; 09/02/67 Gabor
and Albert; 09/06/69 Gabor and
Albert; 08/29/70 Albert.
$8.00 – $12.00 each.

PAPER DOLL BOOKLET #1979, Whitman, 1967.
$35.00 – $45.00.

PAPER DOLL BOX #4773, Whitman, 1968. $35.00 – $45.00.

Other items not pictured:

BOARD GAME, Standard Toykraft, 1965. Photo cover of Lisa and Oliver. $50.00 – $75.00.

COLORING BOOK, Whitman, 1967. Illustration of Oliver, Lisa, and cow at fence. $25.00 – $35.00.

FORDSON TRACTOR, Ertl, 1968. Metal tractor. $75.00 – $100.00.

RECORD/45, "Green Acres"/"Turn Around," Columbia, 1965. Theme from the television show. Vocals by Eddie Albert and Eva Gabor. Without picture sleeve. $5.00 – $8.00.

WRITING TABLET, 1960s. Cover photo of Lisa and Oliver. $15.00 – $20.00.

H.R. PUFNSTUF

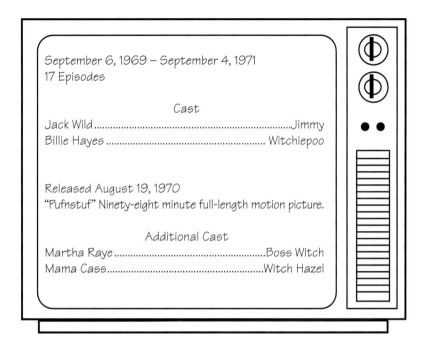

September 6, 1969 – September 4, 1971
17 Episodes

Cast
Jack Wild..Jimmy
Billie Hayes .... Witchiepoo

Released August 19, 1970
"Pufnstuf" Ninety-eight minute full-length motion picture.

Additional Cast
Martha Raye ....Boss Witch
Mama Cass...Witch Hazel

Above and right: BOARD GAME, Milton Bradley, 1971.
$35.00 – $45.00.

COLORING BOOK #1093, Whitman, 1970.
$40.00 – $50.00.

FRAME TRAY PUZZLE #4507, Whitman, 1970.
Witchiepoo's dungeon. $25.00 – $35.00.

Left and below: COMIC BOOKS #1 – 8,
Gold Key/Whitman, 1970 – 1971.
$35.00 – $50.00 #1. $15.00 – $25.00 #2 – 8.

FRAME TRAY PUZZLE #4507, Whitman, 1970.
Witchiepoo's boat. $25.00 – $35.00.

HALLOWEEN COSTUME, Witchiepoo, Collegeville,
1971. $45.00 – $60.00.

JIGSAW PUZZLE #4426, Whitman, 1970.
$40.00 – $50.00.

LUNCH BOX, Aladdin, 1971. Metal box with plastic thermos.
$50.00 – $75.00 box. $25.00 – $35.00 thermos.

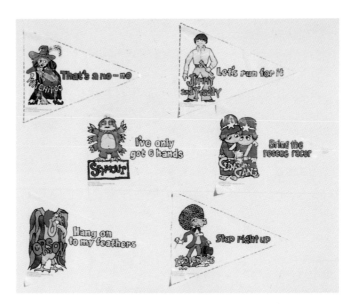

PATCHES, Krofft Productions, 1969. Eight different Kellogg's cereal premiums. Patches are adhesive with paper backings which contain character bios. Pufnstuf, Seymore, and the Four Winds not pictured. $10.00 – $15.00 each.

PENNANTS, Krofft Productions, 1970. Eight different Kellogg's cereal premiums. Plastic pennants came in pairs that required scissors to separate. Pufnstuf and the Four Winds not pictured. $20.00 – $30.00 each pair.

PUPPETS, Remco, 1970. Eight different vinyl puppets. Cling, Jimmy, Orson, and Seymore not pictured. $40.00 – $50.00 each.

TELL-A-TALE BOOK, Whitman, 1970. $15.00 – $20.00.

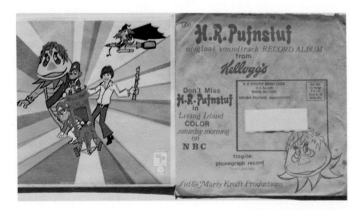

RECORD/45, "H.R. Pufnstuf," Capitol Records, 1970. Fold-open sleeve contains photos of cast and song lyrics. Original soundtrack. Kellogg's mail-away. $35.00 – $45.00.

Other items not pictured:

BELT BUCKLES, 1970s. Two different styles from The World of Sid and Marty Krofft theme park. $20.00 – $25.00 each.

BOP BAG, Coleco, 1970. $40.00 – $50.00.

COMIC BOOK, March of Comics #360, Western Publishing, 1971. $20.00 – $25.00.

FAN CLUB KIT, 1970s. $100.00 – $125.00.

FREDDY THE FLUTE, Kellogg's, 1970s. Plastic flute with movable mouth and instructions. Cereal premium mail-away. $250.00 – $300.00.

FUN RINGS, Kellogg's, 1970s. Eight different premiums. Cling and Clang, Four Winds, Jimmy and Feddy, Ludicrous Lion, Orson, Pufnstuf, Seymore, and Witchiepoo. $30.00 – $35.00 each.

HALLOWEEN COSTUME, Pufnstuf, Collegeville, 1970s. $60.00 – $80.00.

HALLOWEEN COSTUME, Witchiepoo, Collegeville, 1970s. Different version with silk suit and synthetic hair on mask. $45.00 – $60.00.

LOBBY CARDS, Universal Pictures, 1970. Set of eight 11" x 14" cards that feature scenes from the motion picture. $150.00 – $200.00 set.

MUSIC COLORING BOOK, J. Hagg, 1970s. $50.00 – $75.00.

PILLOW DOLL, Pufnstuf, 1970s. $50.00 – $75.00.

POSTERS, Mayor Pufnstuf, Different, and Zap the World. Royal Screen Craft, 1970. Colorful blacklight posters. Each with a scene from the motion picture. $50.00 – $75.00 each.

POSTERS, Universal Pictures, 1970. Cast photos of the motion picture cast. Different sizes. $50.00 – $75.00 each.

PUNCH-OUT BOOK #1922, Whitman, 1970. Illustrated cover with stand-ups inside. $40.00 – $60.00.

PUPPETS, Kellogg's, 1970s. Five different mail-away felt premiums. Cling, Clang, Ludicrous Lion, Pufnstuf, and Witchiepoo. $25.00 – $30.00 each.

RECORD/LP, "Pufnstuf," Capitol Records, 1970. Original Soundtrack of the motion picture. $30.00 – $40.00.

SHEET MUSIC, 1970s. From the motion picture. $15.00 – $20.00.

SOUVENIR MUG, 1970s. Pufnstuf stein from The World of Sid and Marty Krofft theme park. $50.00 – $75.00.

STICKER FUN BOOK, Whitman, 1970s. Illustrated cover. $40.00 – $50.00.

STUFFED DOLL, Pufnstuf, My Toy, 1973. 16" doll. $300.00 – $400.00.

STUFFED DOLL, Witchiepoo, My Toy, 1973. 16" doll. $300.00 – $400.00.

UMBRELLA, 1970s. From The World of Sid and Marty Krofft theme park. $60.00 – $80.00.

HAPPY DAYS

January 15, 1974 – July 19, 1984
256 Episodes
Peak Position: # 1 in the 1976 – 77 season.
Cast:
Henry Winkler............................ Arthur "Fonzie" Fonzarelli
Ron Howard...Richie Cunningham
Tom Bosley...Howard Cunningham
Marion Ross ....Marion Cunningham
Erin Moran..Joanie
Anson Williams...........................Warren "Potsie" Webber
Donny Most ....Ralph Malph

November 1980 – September 1981
13 episodes of Fonz and the Happy Days Gang
animated cartoon.

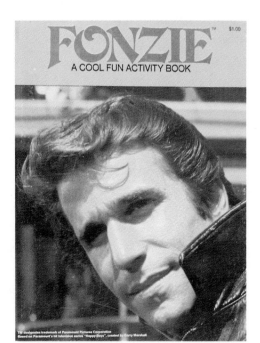

ACTIVITY BOOK, Fonzie, A Cool Fun Activity Book,
Grosset & Dunlap, 1976. $8.00 – $10.00.

BELT, The Fonz and the Happy Days Gang, Paramount, 1981.
$8.00 – $10.00.

BELT BUCKLE, The Fonz, Paramount Pictures
Corp. 1976. Brass finish. $15.00 – $20.00.

Above and right: BOARD GAME, Parker Brothers, 1976.
$10.00 – $15.00.

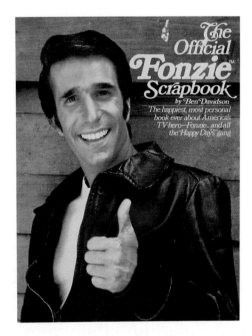

BOOK, *The Official Fonzie Scrapbook*, Grosset &
Dunlap, 1976. $5.00 – $8.00

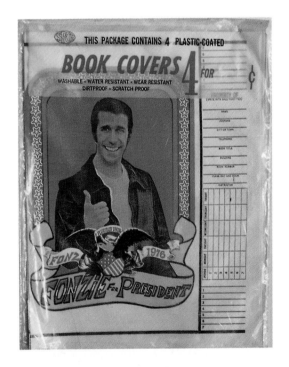

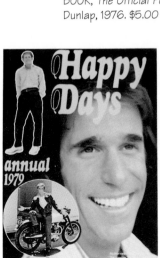

BRITISH ANNUALS, Stafford Pemberton, 1979 – 1981. 1979 pictured.
$15.00 – $20.00 each.

BOOK COVERS, Fonzie, Paramount, 1976. 4 different
in package. $10.00 – $15.00.

BUTTONS, Fonzie, The Pinning Co., 1976. $5.00 – $8.00 each.

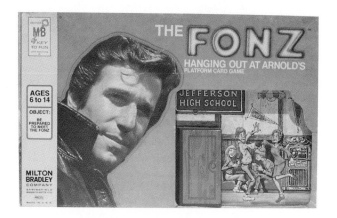

CARD GAME, The Fonz, Hanging Out at Arnold's, Milton Bradley, 1976. $15.00 – $20.00.

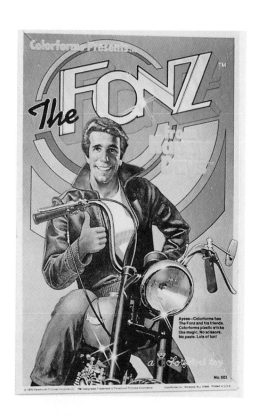

COLORFORMS, The Fonz, Colorforms, 1976. $15.00 – $20.00.

COLORING BOOK, Fonzie, A Cool Coloring Book, Treasure, 1976. $8.00 – $12.00.

COLORING AND ACTIVITY BOOKS, Waldman, 1983. Four different. $8.00 – $12.00 each.

COMIC BOOKS #1 – 6, Gold
Key 1979 – 1980.
    $5.00 – $8.00 each.

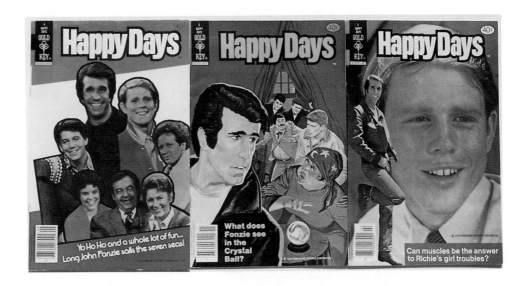

CUP, The Fonz, Paramount,
1977. From Burger King
Restaurants. $5.00 – $8.00.

Right: CUP AND TUM-
BLER, Fonzie, Dawn, 1976.
    $8.00 – $12.00 each.

DOLL, Fonzie, Mego, 1976. Also came in a boxed version. $25.00 – $30.00.

DOLLS, Ralph, Potsie, and Richie, Mego, 1976. $25.00 – $30.00 each.

FLIP-A-KNOT, National Marketing, 1977. Photo of Richie and Joanie on back. $10.00 – $15.00.

HALLOWEEN COSTUME, The Fonz, Ben Cooper, 1976. $15.00 – $20.00.

GLASSES, Libbey Glass Co., 1976. Six in a set. $10.00 – $15.00 each.

JIGSAW PUZZLE, Fonzie,
HG Toys, 1976. In canister.
$10.00 – $15.00.

JIGSAW PUZZLES, HG Toys, 1976. #465-01, #465-02, and #465-03 pictured.
$8.00 – $12.00 each.

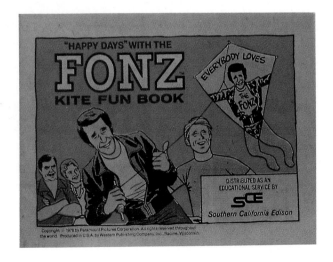

KITE FUN BOOK, Western Publishing, 1978. $8.00 – $12.00.

JIGSAW PUZZLE, The Fonz, HG
Toys, 1976. Giant 250 pieces.
$15.00 – $20.00.

LUNCH BOXES, Thermos, 1977. Two different styles. Same thermos. Metal box with plastic thermos. $25.00 – $30.00 each box; $10.00 – $15.00 thermos.

MIRACLE BUBBLE SHOOTER, The Fonz and the Happy Days Gang, Imperial, 1981. $8.00 – $10.00.

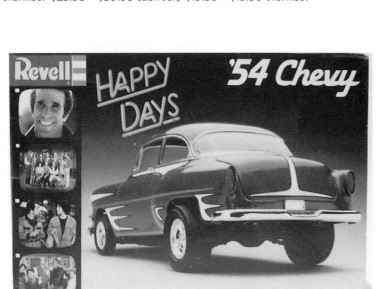

MODEL KIT, '54 Chevy, Revell, 1982. $25.00 – $30.00.

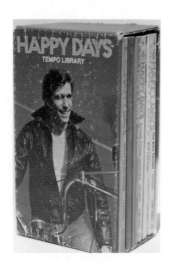

PAPERBACK BOOK SET, Tempo Books, 1976. #1 – 6 in a display box. $25.00 – $30.00.

PAPER DOLL BOX, Fonzie, Toy Factory, 1976. $20.00 – $25.00.

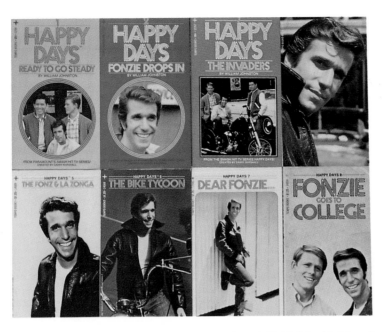

PAPERBACK BOOKS, #1 – 8, Tempo Books, 1974 – 1977. $3.00 – $5.00 each.

PHOTO ALBUM, Gordy, 1983.
$15.00 – $20.00.

PAPERBACK BOOKS, Fonzie, 1976. *The Fonz: The Henry Winkler Story*, Pocket; *The Truth About Fonzie*, Scholastic Books; *The Official Fonzie Scrapbook*, Tempo; *Hollywood's Newest Superstar*, Berkley. $3.00 – $5.00 each.

PINBALL MACHINE, Coleco, 1976. 36" x 20" electric pinball machine. $60.00 – $80.00.

PINS, The Fonz and the Happy Days Gang, Gordy, 1981. Several different. $5.00 – $8.00 each.

PLAY SET, Toy Factory, 1976. $25.00 – $30.00.

RECORD PLAYER, Vanity Fair, 1976. $25.00 – $35.00.

PUFFY STICKERS, The Fonz and the Happy Days Gang, Imperial, 1981. Six different styles. Styles B, C, E, and F pictured. $3.00 – $5.00 each.

POSTER, The Fonz, 1970s. Blacklight poster. $10.00 – $15.00.

RECORD/LP, "Fonzie, Fonzie," London Records, 1976. Children's record with songs about Fonzie. Vocals by the Heyettes. $8.00 – $10.00.

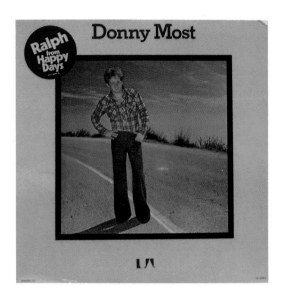

RECORD/LP, "Fonzie Favorites," Ahed, 1976. Compilation of '50s hits. Includes original TV theme and Fonzie phrases. $10.00 – $15.00.

RECORD/LP, "Donny Most," United Artists, 1976. $10.00 – $15.00.

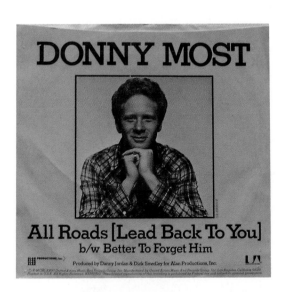

RECORD/45, "All Roads Lead Back to You"/"Better to Forget Him," United Artists, 1976. Vocals by Donny Most. $5.00 – $8.00.

SODA CANS, R. C. Cola, 1978. Numbered set of 35 with different photos. #2 pictured. $5.00 – $8.00 each.

RUB-DOWN TRANSFER GAME, The Fonz and the Happy Days Gang, APC, 1981. Several different. Egyptian Mystery pictured. $5.00 – $8.00 each.

TALKING VIEW-MASTER #AVB586, The Not Making of a President, GAF, 1974. $15.00 – $20.00.

TRADING CARDS SET #1, Topps, 1976. First series has 44 blue-bordered cards and 11 yellow-bordered stickers in set. Cards have puzzle and trivia backs.
  $30.00 – $35.00 set with stickers. $.50 – $.75 single cards.
  $.75 – $1.00 single stickers. $3.00 – $5.00 wrapper.
  $15.00 – $20.00 display box.

TRADING CARDS SET #2, O-Pee-Chee, 1976. Second series has 44 red-bordered cards and 11 red-bordered stickers in set. Cards have puzzle and trivia backs. O-Pee-Chee card sets were made in Canada under license with Topps and are the same as the Topps sets.
  $30.00 – $35.00 set with stickers. $.50 – $.75 single cards.
  $.75 – $1.00 single stickers. $3.00 – $5.00 wrapper.
  $15.00 – $20.00 display box.

THERMOS, The Fonz, Thermos, 1976. $20.00 – $25.00.

TV GUIDES, 1974 – 1984.
06/15/74 Howard and O'Dare;
01/10/76 Howard and Winkler;
01/07/78 Cast; 12/15/79 Winkler;
04/17/82 Winkler, Baio and Moran;
04/23/83 Winkler and Purl;
04/28/84 Cast of 1974 – 1984.
$5.00 – $8.00 each

VIEW-MASTER #B586, The Not Making of a President, GAF, 1974. $10.00 – $15.00.

VIEW-MASTER #J13, Requiem for a Malph, GAF, 1978. $10.00 – $15.00.

Other items not pictured:

BUBB-A-LOONS, The Fonz and the Happy Days Gang, Imperial, 1981. $8.00 – $10.00

CANDY/TRADING CARDS, Fonzie, Phoenix, 1976. Eight cards in set. Cards came as a premium with boxed candy. Photo of Fonzie on box. $20.00 – $30.00 set; $3.00 – $4.00 single cards; $25.00 – $30.00 large display box; $5.00 – $8.00 single boxes..

CHALK STATUE, Fonzie, 1976. $10.00 – $15.00.

FONZ VIEWER, The Fonz and the Happy Days Gang; Larami, 1981. $8.00 – $12.00.

FONZ WALLET, The Fonz and the Happy Days Gang, Larami, 1981. $8.00 – $12.00.

FONZIE'S GARAGE PLAYSET, Mego, 1977. For 8" dolls. $60.00 – $80.00.

FONZIE'S MOTORCYCLE, Mego, 1978. For 8" dolls. $25.00 – $35.00.

GLASSES, Libbey Glass Co., 1977. Set of six with illustration of each character on front and record on back. $20.00 – $30.00 each.

GREETING CARDS, 1970s. Two different boxed styles. $15.00 – $20.00.

GUITAR, Lapin, 1976. Color photo of Fonzie, Richie, and Potsie. $30.00 – $40.00.

HI-BOUNCE BALL, The Fonz and the Happy Days Gang, Imperial, 1981. $8.00 – $10.00.

JALOPY, Mego, 1978. Snap-together hot rod for 8" dolls. Illustration of cast in car on box. $30.00 – $40.00.

JIGSAW PUZZLE, HG Toys, 1974. 500 pieces. Cast photo on box. $20.00 – $25.00.

KNEE-HI NYLONS, 1976. $15.00 – $20.00.

MODEL KIT, Draggin' Wagon, MPC, 1974. Illustration of Fonzie, Richie, and Potsie in car. $30.00 – $40.00.

MODEL KIT, Fonz and his Bike, MPC, 1976. $30.00 – $40.00.

MODEL KIT, Fonzie's Dream Rod, MPC, 1976. Illustration of Fonzie leaning on his car. $30.00 – $40.00.

MODEL KIT, Rock N' Roll Rod, Palmer, 1974. $30.00 – $40.00.

NECKLACE, 1976. Fonz and his motorcycle. $25.00 – $30.00.

PAINT BY NUMBER SET, Craft Master, 1979. Illustration of Fonzie combing his hair on cover. $15.00 – $20.00.

PAPERBACK BOOK, *Henry Winkler and Fonzie*, Zebra Books, 1977. Iron-on inside. $3.00 – $5.00.

POCKET FLIX CASSETTE, Ideal, 1978. *Cassette for the Pocket Flix Viewer.* $8.00 – $12.00.

POSTERS, 1970s. *Several different, including The Fonz and Fonzie for President.* $10.00 – $15.00 each.

RECORD/45, "One of These Days"/"Early Morning," United Artists, 1976. Vocals by Donny Most. Without picture sleeve. $3.00 – $5.00.

RECORD/45, "I Only Want What's Mine"/"Sharing Our Love," Casablanca, 1980. Vocals by Donny Most. With picture sleeve. $5.00 – $8.00.

RECORD/45, "Deeply"/"I Want to Believe In This One," Chelsea, 1977. Vocals by Anson Williams. With picture sleeve. $8.00 – $12.00.

RECORD/45, "Happy Days"/"Crusin' With the Fonz," Reprise Records, 1976. Theme from the television show. Vocals by Pratt and McClain with Brother Love. Without picture sleeve. $3.00 – $5.00.

RUG, Fonzie, 1970s. $10.00 – $15.00.

SHEETS AND PILLOWCASE SET, Fonzie, 1970s. $30.00 – $40.00.

STUFFED DOLL, Fonzie, 1976. 16" doll. $15.00 – $20.00.

TRANSISTOR FIGURAL RADIO, Fonzie, Sutton Associates, 1974. Illustration of Fonzie. $40.00 – $50.00.

T-SHIRTS, 1970s. Various prints of Fonzie. $10.00 – $15.00 each.

WRISTWATCH, Fonzie, Time Trends, 1976. Illustration of Fonzie with a black leather band. $50.00 – $75.00.

THE HARDY BOYS MYSTERIES

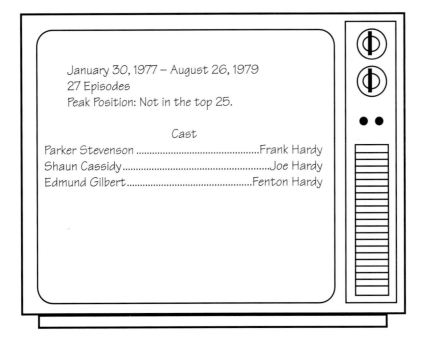

January 30, 1977 – August 26, 1979
27 Episodes
Peak Position: Not in the top 25.

Cast

Parker Stevenson ....Frank Hardy
Shaun Cassidy..Joe Hardy
Edmund Gilbert...Fenton Hardy

Above and right: BOARD GAME, Parker Brothers, 1978.
$10.00 – $15.00.

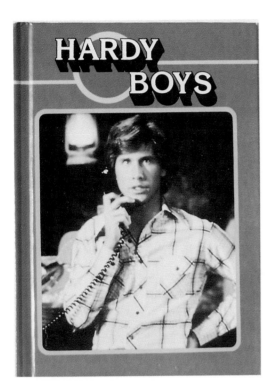

Book, The Hardy Boys, Creative Education, 1979.
$5.00 – $8.00.

BOOKLETS, Tiger Beat, 1970s. Several different. $8.00 – $10.00 each.

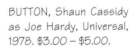

BUTTON, Shaun Cassidy
as Joe Hardy, Universal,
1978. $3.00 – $5.00.

BRITISH ANNUALS, Grandreams, 1977 – 1980.
1980 annual pictured. $10.00 – $15.00 each.

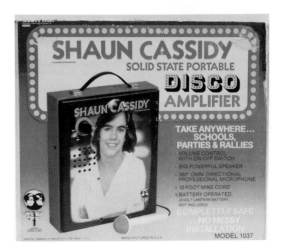

DISCO AMPLIFIER, Shaun Cassidy as Joe Hardy, Vanity
Fair, 1977. $25.00 – $35.00.

DOLLS, Joe Hardy and Frank Hardy, Kenner, 1978. $35.00 – $45.00 each.

GUITAR, Shaun Cassidy as Joe Hardy, Carnival Toys, 1978. $40.00 – $50.00.

JIGSAW PUZZLE, Joe Hardy, APC, 1978. $10.00 – $15.00.

JIGSAW PUZZLE, Joe and Frank Hardy, APC, 1978. $10.00 – $15.00.

LUNCH BOX, K.S.T., 1977. Metal
box with plastic thermos.
$25.00 – $35.00 box.
$10.00 – $15.00 thermos.

MODEL KIT, Revell, 1978. $25.00 – $30.00.

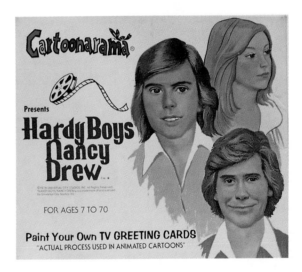

PAINT YOUR OWN TV GREETING CARDS, Cartoonarama,
1978. $30.00 – $40.00.

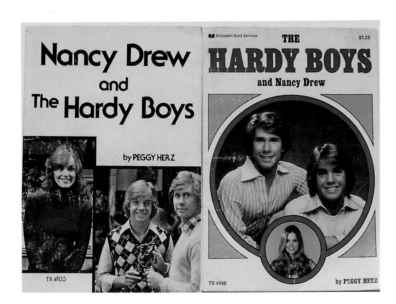

PAPERBACK BOOKS, Nancy Drew and the Hardy Boys
and The Hardy Boys and Nancy Drew, Scholastic, 1977.
$5.00 – $8.00 each.

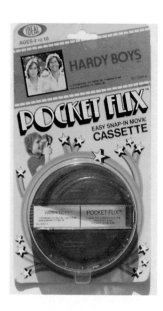

PAPERBACK BOOKS, Mystery Mazes, Detective Logic Puzzles, and Super Sleuth Word Finds, Tempo Books, 1977. $5.00 – $8.00 each.

POCKET FLIX CASSETTE, Ideal, 1978. Cassette for Pocket Flix Viewer. $10.00 – $15.00.

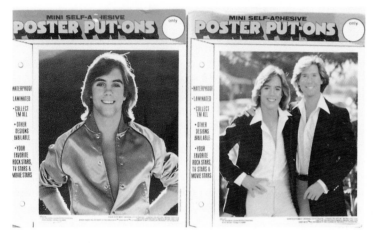

POSTER PUT-ONS, Joe Hardy and Joe and Frank Hardy, Bi-Rite, 1977. $5.00 – $8.00 each.

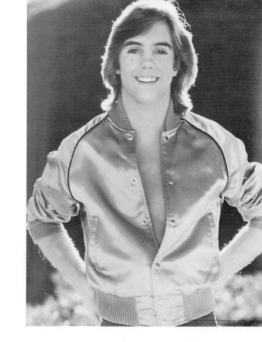

RECORD CASES, Vanity Fair, 1978. Two sizes for LP's and 45's. Case for 45's pictured. $20.00 – $25.00 each.

POSTERS, Pro Arts, 1976. Various styles. Shaun Cassidy as Joe Hardy pictured. $8.00 – $12.00 each.

TV GUIDE.
11/05/77.
$5.00 – $8.00.

T-SHIRTS, Universal, 1977. Various styles. Shaun Cassidy as Joe Hardy pictured. $15.00 – $20.00 each.

Other items not pictured:

CHARM BRACELET, Shaun Cassidy as Joe Hardy, Universal, 1978. $25.00 – $30.00.

FAN CLUB KIT, FCCA, 1977. $25.00 – $35.00.

HALLOWEEN COSTUMES, Joe Hardy and Frank Hardy, Ben Cooper, 1970s. $25.00 – $30.00 each.

IRON-ONS, 1970s. Several styles, including Shaun Cassidy as Joe Hardy and Parker Stevenson as Frank Hardy. $5.00 – $8.00 each.

RECORD/LP, "The Hardy Boys Mysteries," Wonderland, 1978. Photo cover of Joe and Frank Hardy. Narrated adventure stories. $10.00 – $15.00.

RECORD PLAYER, Vanity Fair, 1978. $35.00 – $45.00.

WRISTWATCH, 1970s. Working watch. $50.00 – $60.00.

I DREAM OF JEANNIE

September 18, 1965 – September 8, 1970
139 Episodes
Peak Position: Not in the top 25.

Cast

Barbara Eden ....Jeannie
Larry Hagman ....Major Anthony Nelson
Bill Daly..Major Roger Healey
Hayden Rorke.. Dr. Alfred Bellows
Emmaline Henry......................................Amanda Bellows
Barton MacLane ....General Martin Peterson

September 8, 1973 – September 30, 1975
16 episodes of Jeannie animated cartoon.

Above and right: BOARD GAME, Milton Bradley, 1965.
$40.00 – $50.00.

COMIC BOOKS #1 – 2, Dell, 1966. #1 not pictured. $30.00 – $50.00 each.

DREAMY FASHIONS, Remco, 1977. 36 different outfits for the 6" doll. Fashions came in boxes and on cards. $8.00 – $12.00 each.

DOLL, Jeannie, Remco, 1977. 6" doll. $50.00 – $60.00.

Left: HALLOWEEN COSTUME, Jeannie, Ben Cooper, 1974. From cartoon series.
$20.00 – $25.00.

Right: BOTTLE, Jim Beam, 1964. This line of bottles was decorated for use on the show as Jeannie's bottle.
$50.00 – $75.00.

MAGIC SLATE, Rand McNally, 1975. From cartoon series. $25.00 – $30.00.

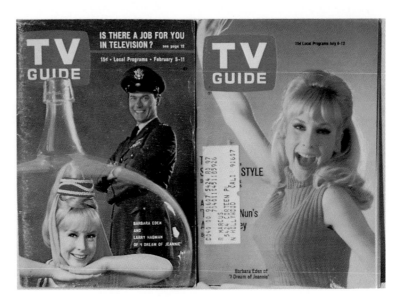

TV GUIDES, 1966 – 1969.
02/05/66 Eden and Hagman; 09/24/66 Eden (not pictured); 07/06/68 Eden; 11/22/69 Eden and Hagman (not pictured).
$10.00 – $15.00 each.

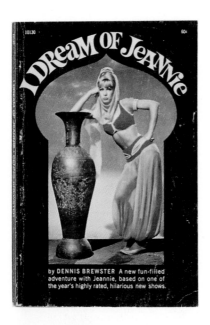

PAPERBACK BOOK, Pocket Books, 1966.
$25.00 – $30.00.

RECORD/LP, "Miss Barbara Eden," Dot, 1967. $40.00 – $60.00.

Other items not pictured:

BOTTLE PLAYSET, Remco, 1977. Playset for the 6" doll. Includes doll in pink outfit. $100.00 – $125.00.

DOLL, Jeannie, Ideal, 1965. 18" doll. $125.00 – $150.00.

DOLL, Jeannie, Libby, 1966. 20" doll. In pink or green outfit. $125.00 – $150.00.

HALLOWEEN COSTUME, Jeannie, Ben Cooper, 1967. $75.00 – $100.00.

JADE JEWELRY, Harmony, 1975. On card with illustration of cartoon Jeannie. $15.00 – $20.00.

KNITTING AND EMBROIDERY KIT, Harmony, 1975. On card with illustration of cartoon Jeannie. $25.00 – $30.00.

PARTY SUPPLIES, Ambassador, 1973. Cups, napkins, plates, and invitations with illustration of cartoon Jeannie. $10.00 – $15.00 each.

PLAYSUIT, Ben Cooper, 1975. Fabric dress-up outfit in box. $30.00 – $45.00.

RECORD/45, "I Wouldn't Be a Fool"/"Bend It!," Dot, 1967. Vocals by Barbara Eden. With picture sleeve. $20.00 – $30.00.

RECORDS/45's, Dot, 1967. "Rebel"/"Heartaches"; "I'm a Fool to Care"/"Pledge of Love." Vocals by Barbara Eden. Without picture sleeves. $10.00 – $15.00 each.

JOSIE AND THE PUSSYCATS

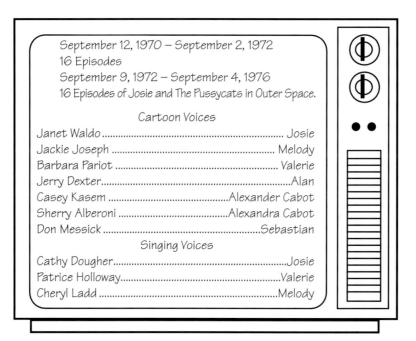

September 12, 1970 – September 2, 1972
16 Episodes
September 9, 1972 – September 4, 1976
16 Episodes of Josie and The Pussycats in Outer Space.

Cartoon Voices

Janet Waldo .... Josie

Jackie Joseph .... Melody

Barbara Pariot .... Valerie

Jerry Dexter...Alan

Casey Kasem ....Alexander Cabot

Sherry Alberoni ....Alexandra Cabot

Don Messick ....……Sebastian

Singing Voices

Cathy Dougher...Josie

Patrice Holloway...Valerie

Cheryl Ladd ....Melody

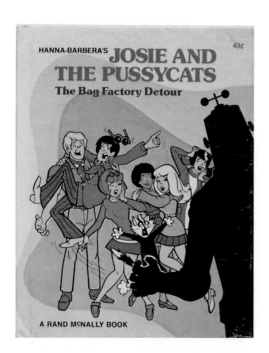

BOOK, *The Bag Factory Detour*, Rand McNally, 1971.
Came in both hardback and softback versions.
$8.00 – $12.00.

COMIC BOOKS, #45 – 106, Radio Comics, 1970 – 1982. #1 – 44 are without
the Pussycats and predate the TV show. #48, 73, and 78 pictured. #55 – 74
are Giant issues with 52 pages. $3.00 – $5.00 each.

CUPS, Radio Comics, 1976. Plastic cups of each character from 7 – 11 convenience stores. Valerie cup pictured. $10.00 – $15.00 each.

GLASS, Hanna-Barbara, 1977. From the Pepsi Collector Series. $15.00 – $20.00.

JIGSAW PUZZLE, Hope, 1972. In canister. European. $25.00 – $35.00.

MUG, Radio Comics, 1971. $8.00 – $12.00.

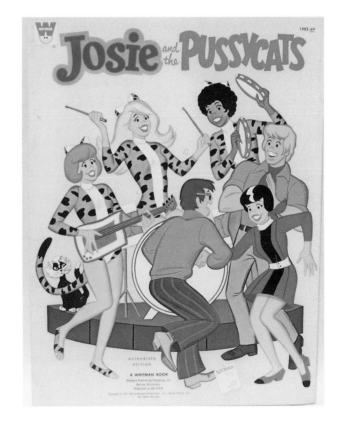

PAPER DOLL BOOKLET #1982, Whitman, 1971. $25.00 – $30.00.

PATCHES, Hanna-Barbara, 1973. Premiums from Wonder Bread. $5.00 – $8.00 each.

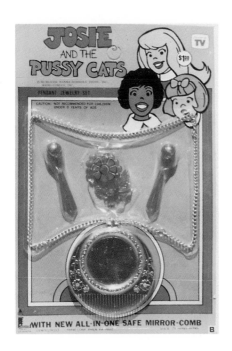

PENDANT JEWELRY SET, Larami, 1972.
$15.00 – $20.00.

PENDANTS, Larami, 1973.
$15.00 – $20.00.

TV CARTOON TATTOOS, Topps, 1971. Hanna-Barbara cartoon tattoos, including Josie and the Pussycats. 16 sheets in a set.
$75.00 – $100.00 set.
$5.00 – $8.00 single sheets.
$3.00 – $5.00 wrapper.
$35.00 – $50.00 display box.

RECORD/LP, "Josie and the Pussycats," Capitol, 1970.
$150.00 – $200.00.

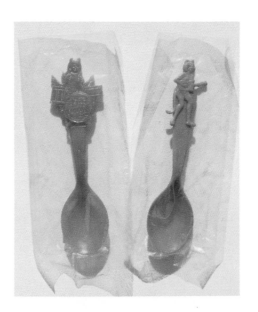

SPOONS, Hanna-Barbara, 1970. Premiums from Honeycomb Cereal. Different characters and colors. $15.00 – $20.00 each.

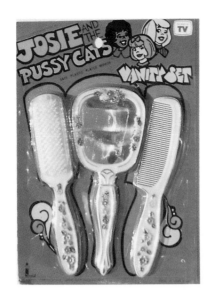

Right: SLICK TICKER PLAY
WATCH, Larami, 1973.
$20.00 – $25.00.

VANITY SET, Larami, 1973.
$20.00 – $25.00.

Other items not pictured:

COLORING BOOK, Rand McNally, 1975. $20.00 – $25.00.

FRAME TRAY PUZZLES, Whitman, 1971. Set of 4 in box. $40.00 – $50.00.

HALLOWEEN COSTUME, Ben Cooper, 1970s. $30.00 – $40.00.

JIGSAW PUZZLE, 1976. Boxed puzzle. $25.00 – $30.00.

MAGIC SLATE, 1971. $25.00 – $30.00.

PENCIL TOPPERS, Hanna-Barbara, 1971. Premiums from Honeycomb Cereal. Different characters. $15.00 – $20.00 each.

RECORDS/45's, Capitol, 1972. "Every Beat of My Heart"/"It's All Right with Me;" "Stop, Look and Listen"/"Say Yeah!." Without picture sleeves. $15.00 – $20.00 each.

RECORDS/45's, Capitol, 1972. The following were available only as Kellogg's mail-away premiums. Each has a picture sleeve. "Inside Outside Upside Down"/"Letter to Mama"; "I Wanna Make You Happy"/"It's Gotta Be Him"; "Every Beat of My Heart"/"Josie" (TV theme); "Voodoo"/"If That Isn't Love." $25.00 – $35.00 each.

STICKERS, 1972. Set of 5 on a card. $15.00 – $20.00.

UNDEROOS UNDERWEAR, 1970s. $15.00 – $20.00.

WRISTWATCH, Bradley, 1970s. Working watch with 3 interchangeable bands. $100.00 – $125.00.

JULIA

September 17, 1968 – May 25, 1971
86 Episodes
Peak Position: #7 in the 1968 – 1969 season.

Cast

Diahann Carroll ....Julia Baker
Lloyd Nolan...Dr. Morton Chegley
Marc Copage ....Corey Baker
Lurene Tuttle ....Hannah Yarby
Michael Link ....Earl J. Waggedorn
Betty Beaird...Marie Waggedorn
Hank Brandt...Len Waggedorn
Fred Williamson......................................Steve Bruce

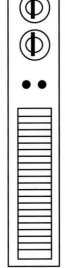

COLORFORMS DRESS-UP KIT, Colorforms, 1969. $20.00 – $25.00.

COLORING BOOK #9523, Saalfied, 1968. Blue or
red cover. $20.00 – $25.00.

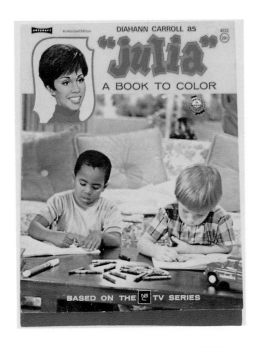

COLORING BOOK #4662, Saalfield, 1969.
$20.00 – $25.00.

PAPER DOLL BOOKLET #5140, Saalfield, 1971.
$30.00 – $35.00.

PAPER DOLL BOX #6055, Saalfield, 1969.
$35.00 – $45.00.

PAPER DOLL BOX #6055, Saalfield, 1969.
$35.00 – $45.00.

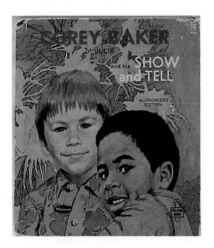

TELL-A-TALE BOOK, *Corey Baker of Julia*, Whitman, 1970. $5.00 – $8.00.

TV GUIDES, 1968 – 1970.
12/14/68 Diahann Carroll; 06/28/69 Cast (not pictured); 03/14/70 Diahann Carroll; 12/26/70 Carroll and Williamson.
$5.00 – $8.00 each.

VIEW-MASTER #B572, GAF, 1969.
$15.00 – $20.00.

Other items not pictured:

ACTIVITY BOX, *Things To Do With Corey and Earl*, Artcraft, 1960s. $35.00 – $45.00.

COLORING BOOK, Saalfield, 1969. Photo cover of Julia with her arms around Corey. $20.00 – $25.00.

DOLL, Julia, Mattel, 1968. Talking 12" doll. Two different versions. $100.00 – $125.00.

HOSPITAL SET, 1960s. Plastic accessories in box. Photo cover of Julia. $50.00 – $75.00.

LUNCH BOX K.S.T., 1969. Metal box with metal thermos. $50.00 – $60.00 box; $25.00 – $30.00 thermos.

PAPER DOLL BOOKLET #4472, Saalfield, 1968. Illustrated cover. $30.00 – $40.00.

PAPER DOLL BOX #6055, Saalfield, 1968. White box with illustrated photos inside squares. $35.00 – $45.00.

PAPER DOLL BOX #6055, Saalfield, 1969. Yellow box with illustration of Julia and children. $35.00 – $45.00.

TRADING CARDS, Topps, 1960s. 33 cards in test issue. No wrapper or box exists. $800.00 – $1,000.00 set; $25.00 – $30.00 single cards.

THE KROFFT SUPERSHOW

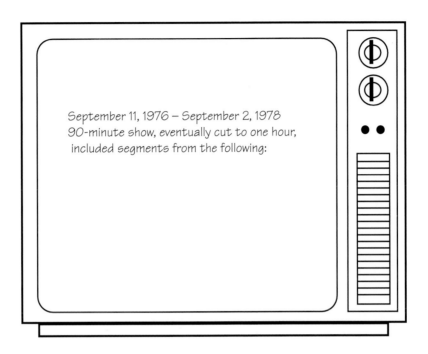

September 11, 1976 – September 2, 1978
90-minute show, eventually cut to one hour,
included segments from the following:

Cast

Kaptain Kool and the Kongs
Michael Lembeck..Kaptain Kool
Debra Clinger ....Superchick
Mickey McMeel...Turkey
Louise Duart...Nashville

Bigfoot and Wildboy
Ray Young...Bigfoot
Joseph Butcher..Wildboy

Dr. Shrinker
Jay Robinson .... Dr. Shrinker
Teddy Eccles ....Brad
Jeff McKay...Gordie
Susan Lawrence...B. J.
Billy Barty..Hugo

Electra Woman and Dyna Girl
Deidre Hall ....Laurie/Electra Woman
Judy Strangis ....Judy/Dyna Girl
Norman Alden .... Frank Heflin

The Lost Saucer
Ruth Buzzi ....Fi
Jim Nabors ....Fum
Larry Larson...Dorse

Wonderbug
John Anthony Bailey..C. C.
David Levy..Barry
Carol Anne Seflinger..Susan

The Krofft Supershow

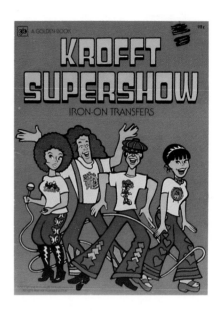

IRON-ON TRANSFERS, Golden Press, 1977. Illustrations of show characters. $15.00 – $20.00.

Left top and center: COMIC BOOKS #1 – 6, Whitman/Gold Key, 1976. $5.00 – $8.00 each.

RECORD/LP, "Stories from the Krofft TV Supershow," Peter Pan, 1978. $10.00 – $15.00.

Other items not pictured:

BOARD GAME, Milton Bradley, 1976. $25.00 – $30.00.

CURTAINS AND BEDSHEET SET, 1978. $40.00 – $50.00.

GOLDEN ALL-STAR BOOK, Golden Press, 1978. $8.00 – $10.00.

LUNCH BOX, Aladdin, 1976. Metal box and plastic thermos. $35.00 – $50.00 box. $15.00 – $20.00 thermos.

Kaptain Kool and the Kongs

FRAME TRAY PUZZLE #T4542-1, Whitman, 1978.
$8.00 – $12.00.

RECORD/LP, "Kaptain Kool and the Kongs," Epic, 1978.
$15.00 – $20.00.

Other items not pictured

BUTTONS, 1977. Two different with cast photos. One of group standing and one with close-up. $5.00 – $8.00 each.

COLOR BY NUMBER SET, 1970s. Cast photo on box. $20.00 – $25.00.

FAN CLUB KIT, Kool Klub, Tiger Beat, 1977. Includes buttons, T-shirt, and posters. $30.00 – $40.00.

JIGSAW PUZZLE, H.G. Toys, 1977. $15.00 – $20.00.

MAGIC SLATE, Whitman, 1970s. Illustration of cast on card. $20.00 – $25.00.

POCKET RADIO, L.J.N., 1977. White with photo of Kaptain Kool and Superchick. $35.00 – $45.00.

POSTER #K-1, 1977. Cast photo. $10.00 – $15.00.

POSTER #K-2, In Concert, 1977. 22" x 34½" shot of group on stage. $10.00 – $15.00.

RECORD/45, "And I Never Dreamed," Epic, 1978. Without picture sleeve. $5.00 – $8.00.

RECORD PLAYER, Vanity Fair, 1978. $35.00 – $45.00.

T-SHIRT, 1977. Photo of group standing with logo above. $15.00 – $20.00.

WRISTWATCH, Kaptain Kool, 1977. Working watch with face featuring photo of Kaptain Kool. $40.00 – $60.00.

Bigfoot and Wildboy

FRAME TRAY PUZZLE #T4542-2, Whitman, 1978. $8.00 – $12.00.

Other items not pictured:

HALLOWEEN COSTUME, Bigfoot, Collegeville, 1978. $30.00 – $40.00.

Dr. Shrinker

JIGSAW PUZZLE, H.G. Toys, 1977. $15.00 – $20.00.

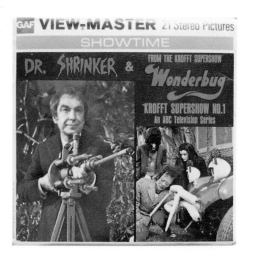

VIEW-MASTER #H2, The Krofft Supershow #1, GAF, 1976. Reel A is Dr. Shrinker and reels B and C are Wonderbug. $15.00 – $20.00.

Other items not pictured:

HALLOWEEN COSTUME, Dr. Shrinker, Ben Cooper, 1976. $30.00 – $40.00.

SHRINK MACHINE, Harmony, 1977. Plastic toy on photo card. $20.00 – $25.00.

Electra Woman and DynaGirl

Above and right: BOARD GAME, Ideal, 1977. $25.00 – $30.00.

HALLOWEEN COSTUME, Electra Woman, Ben Cooper, 1976. $30.00 – $40.00.

Other items not pictured:

JIGSAW PUZZLE, H.G. Toys, 1977. $15.00 – $20.00.

VIEW-MASTER #H3, The Krofft Supershow #2, GAF, 1976. $15.00 – $20.00.

The Lost Saucer
Items not pictured:

BOP BAG, Coleco, 1970s. $30.00 – $40.00.

Wonderbug

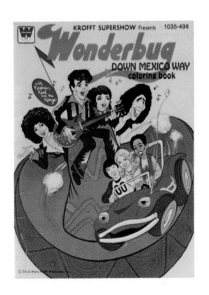

COLORING BOOK #1035, Down Mexico Way, Whitman, 1978. $10.00 – $15.00.

Other items not pictured:

BOARD GAME, Ideal, 1976. Illustration of Schlep car changing into Wonderbug on cover. $25.00 – $30.00.

COLORING BOOK #1066, Rock-A-Bye-Buggy, Whitman, 1978. $10.00 – $15.00.

MAGIC SLATE, Whitman, 1970s. Illustration of Wonderbug and cast. $20.00 – $25.00.

RACE GAME, Harmony, 1977. Carded game with Wonderbug photo at top. $20.00 – $25.00.

KUNG FU

October 14, 1972 – June 27, 1975
72 Episodes
Peak Position: Not in the top 25.

Cast

David Carradine ....Kwai Chang Caine
Keye Luke...Master Po
Philip Ahn ....Master Kan
Radames Pera ....Young Caine "Grasshopper"

BRITISH ANNUALS, Brown Watson, 1972 – 1975. 1975
annual pictured. $10.00 – $15.00 each.

HALLOWEEN COSTUME, Caine, Ben Cooper, 1973.
$20.00 – $25.00.

LUNCH BOX, K.S.T., 1974. Metal box with plastic thermos.
$35.00 – $45.00 box. $10.00 – $15.00 thermos.

PAPERBACK BOOKS, #1 – 4, Warner,
1974. $3.00 – $5.00 each.

RECORD/LP, "Kung Fu," Warner Bros., 1973. $20.00 – $25.00.

VIEW-MASTER #B598, GAF, 1974. $15.00 – $20.00.

TRADING CARDS, Topps, 1973. 60 cards in set. Cards 1 – 44 have puzzle backs
and 45 – 60 include Kung Fu trivia.

$60.00 – $80.00 set. $1.00 – $1.50 single cards.

$5.00 – $8.00 wrapper. $40.00 – $50.00 display box.

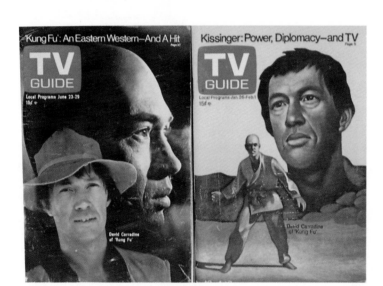

TV GUIDES, 1973 – 1974.
06/23/73 Carradine; 01/26/74
Carradine illustrated
$5.00 – $8.00 each.

Other items not pictured:

CIGAR BANDS, 1970s. European set of 24. $50.00 – $60.00.

JIGSAW PUZZLE, 1975. In canister. $10.00 – $15.00.

RECORD/LP, "Grasshopper," Jet, 1975. European. $30.00 – $35.00.

TALKING VIEW-MASTER #AVB598, GAF, 1973. $20.00 – $25.00.

TARGET SET, Multiple Toymaker, 1970s. On card. $20.00 – $25.00.

LAND OF THE LOST

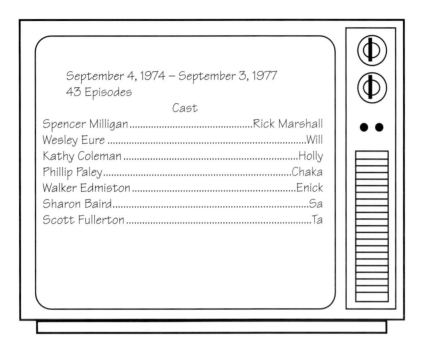

September 4, 1974 – September 3, 1977
43 Episodes

Cast

Spencer Milligan ....Rick Marshall
Wesley Eure ....Will
Kathy Coleman ....Holly
Phillip Paley..Chaka
Walker Edmiston...Enick
Sharon Baird..Sa
Scott Fullerton...Ta

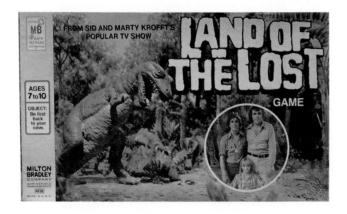

Above and right: BOARD GAME, Milton Bradley, 1975.
$20.00 – $25.00.

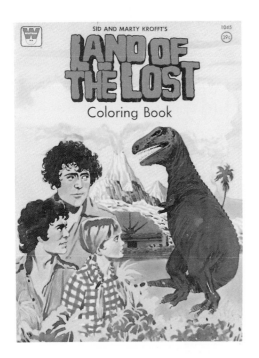

COLORING BOOK #1045, Whitman, 1975.
$15.00 – $20.00.

COSMIC SIGNAL, Larami, 1975.
$15.00 – $20.00.

MOON SPINNERS, Larami, 1975.
$15.00 – $20.00.

JIGSAW PUZZLE #4609, Whitman, 1975.
$15.00 – $20.00.

LITTLE GOLDEN BOOK, *The Surprise Guests*,
Golden Press, 1975. $8.00 – $10.00.

LUNCH BOX, Aladdin, 1975. Metal box with plastic thermos. Back of box pictured.
$50.00 – $60.00 box. $20.00 – $25.00 thermos.

SAFARI SHOOTER, Larami, 1975.
$20.00 – $25.00.

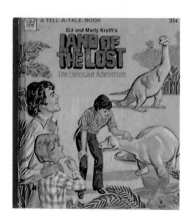

SECRET LOOK-OUT, Larami,
1975. $15.00 – $20.00.

SPARK SHOOTER, Larami,
1975. $15.00 – $20.00.

TELL-A-TALE BOOK, *The Dinosaur Adventure*, Whitman, 1975. $8.00 – $10.00.

VIEW-MASTER #H1, Abominable Snowman, GAF, 1977.
$15.00 – $20.00.

Other items not pictured:

COLOR AND ACTIVITY BOOK #1271, Whitman, 1975. Illustrated cover. $15.00 – $20.00.

EXPLORER'S KIT, Larami, 1975. $20.00 – $25.00.

GIVE-A-SHOW PROJECTOR, Kenner, 1975. $35.00 – $45.00.

HALLOWEEN COSTUME, Rick Marshall, Ben Cooper, 1974. $40.00 – $60.00.

HALLOWEEN COSTUME, Sleestak, Ben Cooper, 1975. $40.00 – $60.00.

PLASTIC DINOSAURS, Larami, 1975. $15.00 – $20.00.

TALKING VIEW-MASTER #TH1, GAF, 1977. $25.00 – $30.00.

VIEW-MASTER #B579, GAF, 1974. $20.00 – $25.00.

LAVERNE AND SHIRLEY

January 27, 1976 – May 10, 1983
178 Episodes
Peak Position: #1 in the 1977 – 1979 seasons.

Cast

Penny Marshall..Laverne DeFazio
Cindy Williams..Shirley Feeney
Phil Foster...Frank DeFazio
David L. Lander ....Andrew "Squiggy" Squigman
Michael McKean..Lenny Kosnowski
Betty Garrett..Edna Babbish
Eddie Mekka..Carmine Ragusa

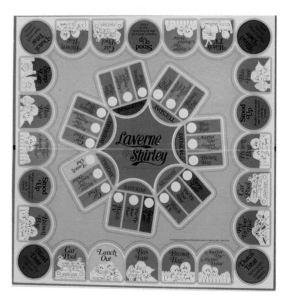

Above and right: BOARD GAME, Parker Brother, 1977.
$15.00 – $20.00.

COLORING AND ACTIVITY BOOKS, Waldman, 1983.
Four different. $8.00 – $10.00 each.

DOLLS, Laverne and Shirley, Mego, 1977.
$80.00 – $100.00.

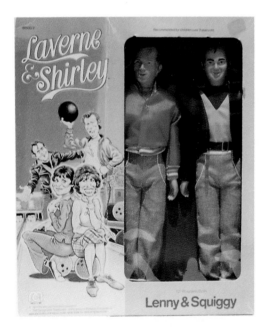

DOLLS, Lenny and Squiggy, Mego, 1977.
$100.00 – $120.00.

JIGSAW PUZZLES, HG Toys, 1976. Three different. #425-02 and #425-03
pictured. $8.00 – $12.00 each.

HALLOWEEN COSTUME, Laverne, Collegeville, 1977.
$25.00 – $30.00.

HALLOWEEN COSTUME, Shirley, Collegeville, 1977.
$25.00 – $30.00.

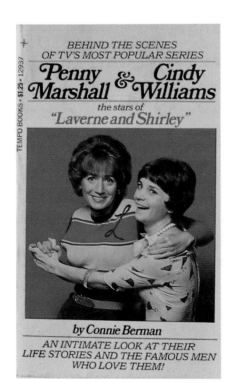

PAPERBACK BOOKS, #1 – 3, Warner Books, 1976. $5.00 – $10.00 each.

PAPERBACK BOOK, Penny Marshall and Cindy
Williams, Tempo Books, 1977. $5.00 – $8.00.

POCKETBOOK PURSE, Harmony, 1977.
$10.00 – $15.00.

RECORD/LP, "Laverne and Shirley Sing," Atlantic Records, 1976.
$10.00 – $15.00.

RECORD/LP, "Lenny and Squiggy Present Lenny and the Squigtones,"
Casablanca Records, 1979. Includes poster inside. $15.00 – $20.00.

SECRETARY SET, Harmony, 1977.
$10.00 – $15.00.

SHEET MUSIC, "Sixteen Reasons," Big 3, 1976.
$8.00 – $12.00.

TV GUIDES, 1976 – 1982.
05/22/76 Marshall and Williams; 06/18/77 Marshall and Williams illustrated; 04/29/78 Cast; 05/19/79 Marshall and Williams illustrated; 08/28/82 Marshall and Williams.
$5.00 – $8.00 each.

VIEW-MASTER #J20, The Slow Child, GAF, 1978.
$10.00 – $15.00.

Other items not pictured:

POCKET FLIX CASSETTE, Ideal, 1978. Cassette for the Pocket Flix Viewer. $10.00 – $15.00.

RECORDS/45's, Atlantic Records, 1976. "Chapel of Love"/"Sixteen Reasons"; "Da Doo Ron Ron"/"Five Years On"; "Graduation Day"/"All I Have to Do is Dream." Vocals by Penny Marshall and Cindy Williams. Without picture sleeves. $5.00 – $8.00 each.

TIGER CLAW PENDANT, Harmony, 1977. $10.00 – $15.00.

WATCH AND POCKET PIN, Harmony, 1977. $10.00 – $15.00.

LIDSVILLE

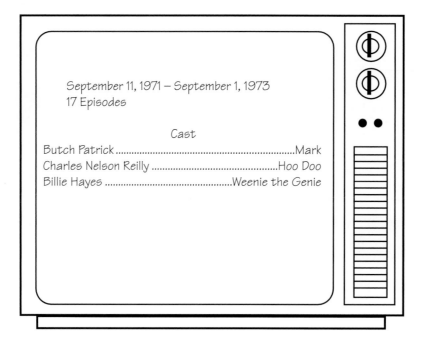

September 11, 1971 – September 1, 1973
17 Episodes

Cast

Butch Patrick ....Mark
Charles Nelson Reilly ....Hoo Doo
Billie Hayes ....Weenie the Genie

COMIC BOOKS, #1 – 5, Whitman/Gold Key 1972 – 1973. #4 not pictured. $10.00 – $15.00 each.

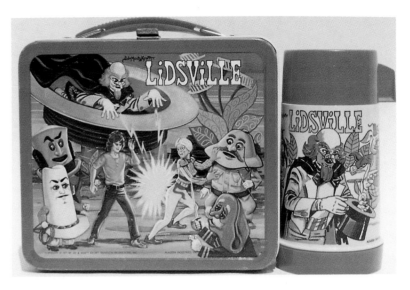

DOT BOOK #1266, Whitman, 1973.
$25.00 – $30.00.

LUNCH BOX, Aladdin, 1971. Metal box with plastic thermos.
$40.00 – $60.00 box. $25.00 – $30.00 thermos.

Other items not pictured:

BOARD GAME, Milton Bradley, 1971. $35.00 – $45.00.

HALLOWEEN COSTUME, Hoo Doo, Collegeville, 1970s. $40.00 – $60.00.

HALLOWEEN COSTUME, Weenie the Genie, Collegeville, 1970s. $40.00 – $60.00.

THE LIFE AND TIMES OF GRIZZLY ADAMS

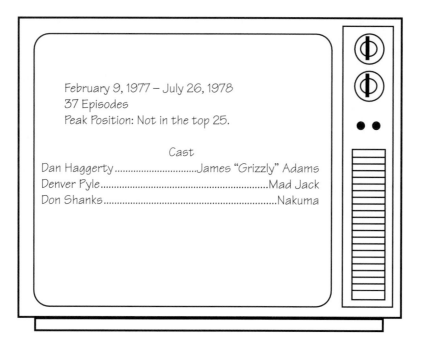

February 9, 1977 – July 26, 1978
37 Episodes
Peak Position: Not in the top 25.

Cast
Dan Haggerty.............................James "Grizzly" Adams
Denver Pyle..Mad Jack
Don Shanks..Nakuma

DOLL, Grizzly Adams, Mattel, 1978.
$25.00 – $30.00.

PAPERBACK BOOK, Sunn, 1977.
$3.00 – $5.00.

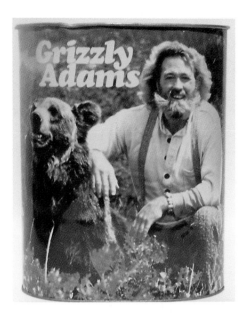

TRASH CAN, Chienco, 1977. $20.00 – $25.00.

TV GUIDES, 1977 – 1978.
06/11/77 Haggerty; 01/28/78 Haggerty illustrated.
$3.00 – $5.00 each.

VIEW-MASTER #J10, GAF, 1978. $10.00 – $15.00.

Other items not pictured:

BOARD GAME, Save the Animals, Waddingtons, 1978. $20.00 – $25.00.

BOARD GAME, House of Games, 1978. $20.00 – $25.00.

COLORING BOOK, Rand McNally, 1978. $10.00 – $15.00.

DOLL, Nakoma, Mattel, 1978. $25.00 – $30.00.

DOLL, Grizzly Adams and Ben Set, Mattel, 1978. $50.00 – $60.00.

JIGSAW PUZZLES, HG Toys, 1978. Three different. $8.00 – $12.00 each.

JIGSAW PUZZLE, House of Games, 1978. Boxed with photo cover of Grizzly Adams and Ben. $8.00 – $12.00.

LUNCH BOX, Aladdin, 1977. Metal dome box with plastic thermos. $50.00 – $60.00 box; $20.00 – $25.00 thermos.

STUFFED MULE, 1970s. Grizzly Adams written on saddle. $25.00 – $30.00.

LITTLE HOUSE ON THE PRAIRIE

September 11, 1974 – September 21, 1982
216 Episodes
Peak Position: #7 in the 1977 – 1978 season.

Cast

Michael Landon ....Charles Ingalls
Karen Grassle...Caroline Ingalls
Melissa Sue Anderson ....Mary
Melissa Gilbert...Laura
Lindsay/Sidney Greenbush ....Carrie
Victor French ....Isaiah Edwards
Richard Bull..Nels Oleson
Katherine MacGregor ....Harriet Oleson
Alison Arngrim...Nellie
Jonathon Gilbert...Willie

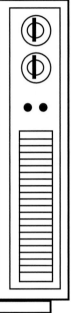

Above and right: BOARD GAME, Parker Brothers, 1978.
$15.00 – $20.00.

COLORFORMS, Colorforms, 1978. $25.00 – $35.00.

DOLLS, Laura and Carrie, Knickerbocker, 1978. $35.00 – $45.00 each.

JIGSAW PUZZLE #490-5, HG Toys, 1978. $10.00 – $15.00.

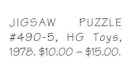

HALLOWEEN COSTUME, Laura, Ben Cooper, 1970s. $15.00 – $20.00.

LUNCH BOX, Thermos, 1978. Metal box with plastic thermos.
$30.00 – $45.00 box. $15.00 – $20.00 thermos.

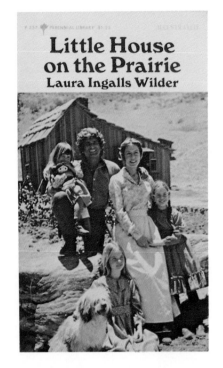

PAPERBACK BOOK, Perennial Library, 1975.
$3.00 - $5.00.

TV GUIDES, 1974 – 1982.
12/07/74 Landon; 06/07/75 Cast illustrated; 05/29/76 Cast; 05/13/78 Cast illustrated; 07/14/79 Landon, Boomer, and Anderson; 07/05/80 Cast illustrated;
01/09/82 Landon illustrated.
$5.00 – $8.00 each.

THREE-RING BINDER, JLM, 1979.
$10.00 – $15.00.

Other items not pictured:

PAINT BY NUMBER SET, Craft House, 1979. Illustration of family on box.
$25.00 – 35.00.

THE LOVE BOAT

September 29, 1977 – September 5, 1986
255 Episodes
Peak Position: #5 in the 1980 – 1981 season.

Cast

Gavin MacLeod	Captain Merrill Stubing
Bernie Kopell	Adam "Doc" Bricker
Fred Grandy	Burl "Gopher" Smith
Ted Lange	Isaac Washington
Lauren Tewes	Julie McCoy
Jill Whelan	Vicki

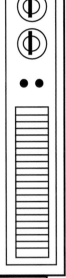

Above and right: BOARD GAME, World Cruise, Ungame, 1980.
$15.00 – $20.00.

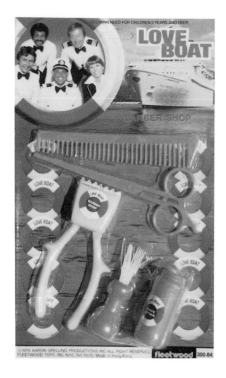

BARBER SET, Fleetwood, 1979.
$8.00 – $12.00.

FIGURES, Captain Stubing, Doc, Gopher, Isaac, Julie, and Vicki,
Mego, 1981. $8.00 – $10.00 each.

JIGSAW PUZZLE, #490-03, HG Toys, 1978. $10.00 – $15.00.

LOVE BOAT IN PORT, Fleetwood, 1979.
$8.00 – $12.00.

PORCELAIN PLATE, Schmid, 1984.
$30.00 – $40.00.

TAKE-A-TRIP, Imperial, 1983.
$8.00 – $12.00.

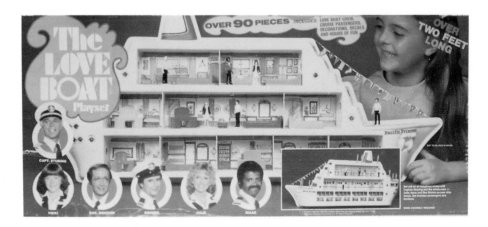

PLAYSET, Multi-Toys, Inc., 1983. $60.00 – $80.00.

REPLICA MODEL, Montego, 1984. $15.00 – $20.00.

TRAVEL BAG, Imperial, 1983. $8.00 – $12.00.

TV GUIDES, 1978 – 1984.
02/04/78 Cast illustrated; 07/22/78 MacLeod; 07/19/80 Cast
illustrated; 06/05/82 Tewes and MacLeod illustrated; 12/24/84
Cast illustrated. $5.00 – $8.00 each.

Other items not pictured:

DOCTOR'S KIT, Imperial, 1983. $8.00 – $12.00.

PUFFY STICKERS, Imperial, 1980s. $5.00 – $8.00.

RECORD/45, "Love Boat Theme"/"The Rockford Files," Polydor, 1979. Theme from
the television show. Side A vocals by Jack Jones. Side B instrumentals by Mike
Post. $3.00 – $5.00.

THE MOD SQUAD

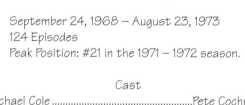
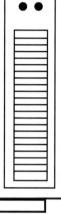

September 24, 1968 – August 23, 1973
124 Episodes
Peak Position: #21 in the 1971 – 1972 season.

Cast

Michael Cole ....Pete Cochrane
Clarence Williams III ....Linc Hayes
Peggy Lipton ....Julie Barnes
Tige Williams ....Captain Adam Greer

BOOKS, Whitman, 1969 – 1970. Assignment: The Arranger;
Assignment: The Hideout. $5.00 – $8.00 each.

JIGSAW PUZZLE #4089, Milton Bradley, 1969.
$30.00 – $35.00.

COMIC BOOKS, #1 – 8 Dell,
1969 – 1971. #2 and 6 not pictured.
$15.00 – $20.00 #1.
$10.00 – $15.00 #2 – 8.

PAPERBACK BOOKS, #1 – 5, Pyramid Books,
1968 – 1970. $5.00 – $8.00 each.

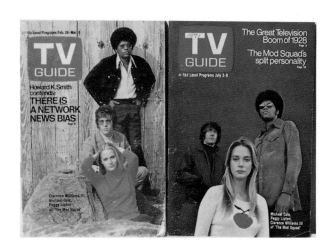

TRADING CARDS, Topps, 1968. 55 cards in the set with puzzle backs.
$110.00 – $150.00 set. $2.00 – $3.00 single cards.
$35.00 – $45.00 wrapper. $75.00 – $100.00 display box.

TV GUIDES, 1968 – 1970.
11/02/68 Cast (not pictured); 07/12/69 Cast (not pictured); 02/28/70 Cast; 07/03/71 Cast.
$8.00 – $12.00 each.

VIEW-MASTER #B478 GAF, 1968.
$20.00 – $25.00.

Other items not pictured:

BOARD GAME, Remco, 1968. $50.00 – $75.00.

JIGSAW PUZZLE, Milton Bradley, 1969. Cast photo with paisley background. $30.00 – $35.00.

MODEL KIT, Station Wagon, Aurora, 1969. $100.00 – $125.00.

RECORD/LP, "Peggy Lipton," Ode Records, 1968. $15.00 – $25.00.

RECORD/45, "Stoney End"/"San Francisco Glide," Ode Records, 1969. Vocals by Peggy Lipton. With picture sleeve. $10.00 – $15.00.

RECORDS/45's, Ode Records, 1969. "Wear Your Love Like Heaven"/"Honey Won't Let Me"; "Red Clay County Line"/"Just a Little Lovin'"; "Lu"/"Let Me Pass By." Vocals by Peggy Lipton. Without picture sleeves. $5.00 – $10.00 each.

MORK AND MINDY

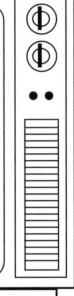

September 14, 1978 – August 5, 1982
91 Episodes
Peak Position: #3 in the 1978 – 1979 season.

Cast

Robin Williams...Mork
Pam Dawber ....Mindy McConnell
Conrad Janis...Fred McConnell
Tom Poston..Frank Bickley
Elizabeth Kerr...Cora Hudson
Robert Donner ....Exidor
Ralph James ....Orson

4-WHEEL DRIVE JEEP, Mattel, 1979. For 8" dolls. $35.00 – $45.00.

ACTIVITY BOOK, Na-No! Na-No!, Wonder Books, 1979. $8.00 – $10.00.

ACTIVITY BOOK, The Mork and Mindy Activity Book, Wonder Books, 1979. $8.00 – $10.00.

ACTIVITY BOOK, The Mork Book of Orkian Fun, Wonder Books, 1979. $8.00 – $10.00.

ACTIVITY BOOK, Mork from Ork, Wonder Books, 1979. $8.00 – $10.00.

BOOK, The Official Mork and Mindy Scrapbook, Wallaby, 1979. $5.00 – $8.00.

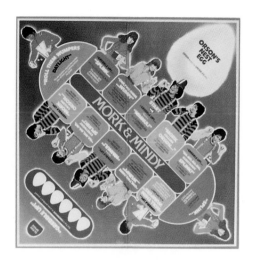

Above and right: BOARD GAME, Milton Bradley, 1979.
$10.00 – $15.00.

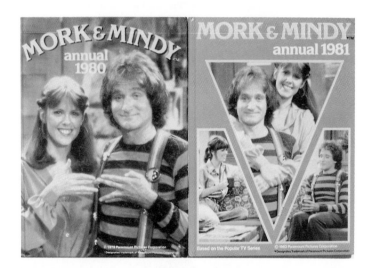

BRITISH ANNUALS, Stafford Pemberton, 1980 – 1981.
$10.00 – $15.00 each.

BUTTONS, Paramount, 1979.
Several different.
$5.00 – $8.00 each.

CARD GAME, Milton Bradley, 1978.
$10.00 – $15.00.

COLORFORMS, Colorforms, 1979. $10.00 – $15.00.

COLORFORMS, Stand Up Play Set, Colorforms, 1979. $10.00 – $15.00.

FIGURINE PAINTING SET, Milton Bradley, 1979. $10.00 – $15.00.

DOLLS, Mork and Mindy, Mattel, 1979. $25.00 – $30.00 each.

HALLOWEEN COSTUME, Mork, Ben Cooper, 1978. $15.00 – $20.00.

JIGSAW PUZZLES, Milton Bradley, 1978. Four different. #4 pictured. $8.00 – $10.00 each.

LUNCH BOX, Thermos, 1978. Metal box with plastic thermos. $20.00 – $25.00 box. $8.00 – $12.00 thermos.

MITTENS, PPC, 1979. $10.00 – $15.00.

LUNCH BOX, Thermos, 1978. Plastic box with plastic thermos. $20.00 – $25.00 box. $8.00 – $12.00 thermos.

PAPERBACK BOOK, *Mork and Mindy: A Video Novel*, Pocket Books, 1978. $5.00 – $8.00.

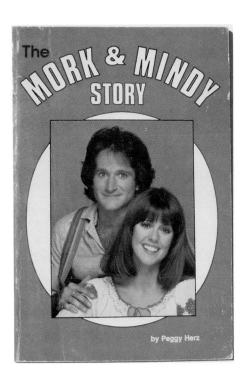

PAPERBACK BOOK, *The Mork and Mindy Story*, Scholastic, 1979. $3.00 – $5.00.

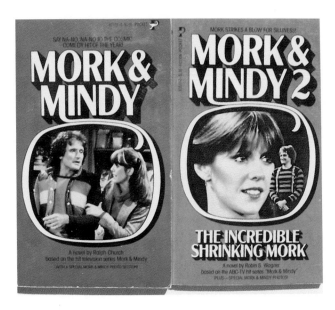

PAPERBACK BOOKS, #1 – 2, Pocket Books, 1979 – 1980. $3.00 – $5.00 each.

PAPERBACK BOOKS, *Mork and Mindy Puzzlers* and *Code Puzzles From Ork*, Cinnamon House, 1979. $5.00 – $8.00 each.

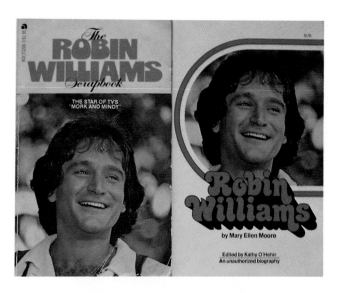

PAPERBACK BOOKS, *The Robin Williams Scrapbook* and *Robin Williams*, Grosset and Dunlap, 1979. *$3.00 – $5.00 each.*

PARTY SUPPLIES, Ambassador, 1979. Includes cups, plates, napkins, and tablecloth. Plates and napkins pictured. *$5.00 – $8.00 each.*

PATCHES, Aviva, 1979. *Several different styles.*
$3.00 – $5.00 each.

RADIO, Concept 2000, 1979. *$25.00 – $35.00.*

SPIRAL NOTEBOOK, Stuart Hall, 1979.
$5.00 – $8.00.

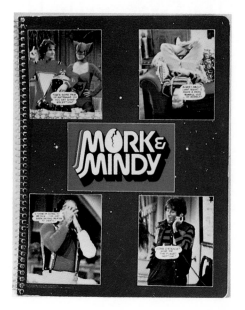

STICKERS, Aviva, 1979. Several different styles. $3.00 – $5.00 each.

TALKING RAG DOLL, Mork, Mattel, 1979.
$15.00 – $20.00.

TRADING CARDS, Topp, 1978. 99 cards and 22 stickers in set. 55 cards have
puzzle backs and 44 have trivia.

    $20.00 – $25.00 set with stickers.
    $.25 – $.50 single stickers.
    $8.00 – $10.00 display box.

    $.15 – $.25 single cards.
    $1.00 – $2.00 wrapper.

VIEW-MASTER #K67, GAF, 1979.
$10.00 – $15.00.

TV GUIDES, 1978 – 1980.
10/28/78 Dawber and Williams; 05/03/80 Dawber and Williams illustrated; 11/22/80 Dawber.
$3.00 – $5.00 each.

Other items not pictured:

WINDOW DECALS, Aviva, 1979. Several different styles.
$5.00 – $8.00 each.

BELT, Mork from Ork, PPC, 1979. Children's leather belt. $10.00 – $15.00.

BUBBLE GUM IN EGG, Amurol Products Co., 1978. $20.00 – $25.00 full box; $10.00 – $15.00 empty box.

FIGURE, Mork in Egg Spaceship, Mattel, 1979. $10.00 – $15.00.

FLICKER RINGS, 1970s. Several styles, including Mork and Shazbot. $8.00 – $10.00 each.

GUMBALL BANK, Mork, Hasbro, 1980. Figural Mork sits on top of bank. $20.00 – $25.00.

MAGIC SHOW PLAYSET, Colorforms, 1980. $20.00 – $25.00.

MAGIC TRANSFER SET, 1979. $10.00 – $15.00.

MODEL KIT, Jeep, Mono, 1979. $20.00 – $25.00.

PAINT BY NUMBERS SET, Craft Master, 1979. $10.00 – $15.00.

SHEET MUSIC, Theme, 1970s. With photo cover. $5.00 – $8.00.

SHRINKY DINKS, Colorforms, 1979. $10.00 – $15.00.

SLEEPING BAG, Mork, Paramount, 1979. $20.00 – $25.00.

TALKING ALARM CLOCK, Concept 2000, 1980. Figural Mork sits along side of clock. $30.00 – $40.00.

WRISTWATCH, 1970s. $30.00 – $40.00.

NANNY AND THE PROFESSOR

January 21, 1970 – December 27, 1971
54 Episodes
Peak Position: Not in the top 25.

Cast

Juliet Mills ....Phoebe "Nanny" Figalilly
Richard Long ....Professor Harold Everett
David Doremus ....Hal
Trent Lehman ....Butch
Kim Richards ....Prudence

CARTOON KIT, Colorforms, 1971.
$25.00 – $35.00.

COLORING BOOK #3835, Saalfield, 1971.
$20.00 – $25.00.

COLORING BOOK #3929, Saalfield, 1971.
$20.00 – $25.00.

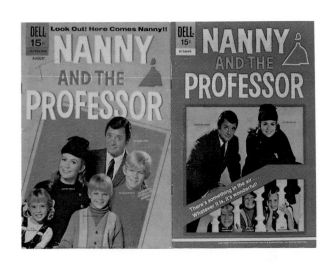

COMIC BOOKS, #1 – 2, Dell, 1970.
$15.00 – $20.00 each.

PAPER DOLL BOOKLET #1213, Saalfield, 1970.
$25.00 – $35.00.

PAPER DOLL BOOKLET #4283, Artcraft, 1971.
$25.00 – $35.00.

PAPER DOLL BOOKLET #5114, Artcraft, 1971.
$25.00 – $35.00.

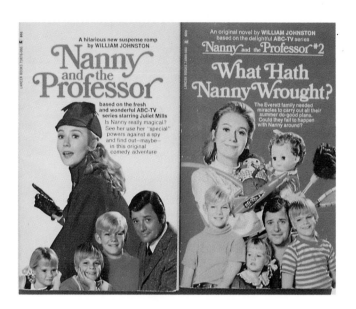

PAPERBACK BOOKS, #1 – 2, Lancer Books, 1970.
$8.00 – $10.00 each.

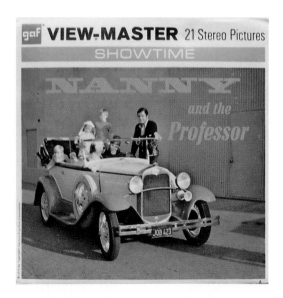

VIEW-MASTER #B573, GAF, 1970. $25.00 – $30.00.

THE NEW ZOO REVUE

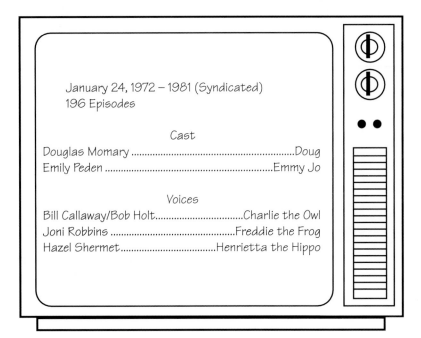

January 24, 1972 – 1981 (Syndicated)
196 Episodes

Cast

Douglas Momary ....Doug
Emily Peden ....Emmy Jo

Voices

Bill Callaway/Bob Holt.............................Charlie the Owl
Joni Robbins ....Freddie the Frog
Hazel Shermet..................................Henrietta the Hippo

BENDIES, 1970s. Bendable figures of
Charlie, Henrietta, and Freddie. Henrietta pictured. $10.00 – $15.00 each.

BOARD GAME, The New Zoo Revue Friendship Game, Kontrell, 1973.
$20.00 – $25.00.

Above and right: BOARD GAME, Ungame, 1981. Christian and non-Christian versions. $15.00 – $20.00.

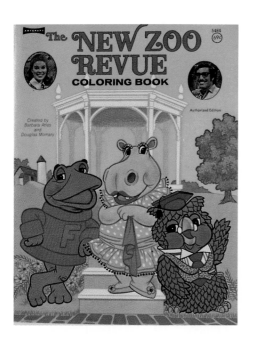

Right: COLORING BOOK #C0544, Saalfield, 1973. $15.00 - $20.00.

COLORING BOOK #5484, Artcraft, 1973. $15.00 – $20.00.

ERASERS, Diener Ind., 1972. $20.00 – $25.00.

LUNCH BOX, Aladdin, 1975. Vinyl box with plastic thermos.
$150.00 – $200.00 box. $20.00 – $25.00 thermos.

PAPER DOLL BOX, Henrietta, Saalfield,
1974. $20.00 – $25.00.

MUSICAL MOBILE, 1970s. $30.00 – $40.00.

PRESS-OUT ALBUM, Artcraft, 1974.
$25.00 - $30.00.

RECORD/LP, "New Zoo Revue," #3807, Disneyland Records, 1972. Cover opens into an eleven-page booklet.
$20.00 – $25.00.

RECORD/LP, "New Zoo Revue," #1344, Disneyland Records, 1972.
$15.00 – $20.00.

STUFFED DOLL, Freddie, Rushton, 1970s.
$30.00 – $35.00.

STUFFED DOLL, Freddie, Kamar, 1977.
$25.00 – $30.00.

STUFFED DOLL, Henrietta, 1970s.
$25.00 – 30.00.

VIEW-MASTER #B566, GAF, 1972.
$15.00 – $20.00.

Other items not pictured:

VIEW-MASTER #B567, GAF, 1974.
$15.00 – $20.00.

BOARD GAME, Cadaco, 1981. $15.00 – $20.00.

COLORING BOOK, Artcraft, 1974. 3 square photos. One with Henrietta holding a parasol. $15.00 – $20.00.

COLORING BOOK, Saalfield, 1974. Illustration of Henrietta, Freddie, and Charlie near tree. $15.00 – $20.00.

FIGURES, 1970s. Charlie, Freddie, Henrietta, and Freida. $10.00 – $15.00 each.

HALLOWEEN COSTUME, Freddie, 1970s. $35.00 – $45.00.

HAND PUPPETS, Henrietta and Freddie, 1970s. $25.00 – $30.00 each.

PAPER DOLL BOOKLET, Henrietta, Saalfield, 1974. Same cover as boxed version. $20.00 – $25.00.

STUFFED DOLLS, 1970s. Other character dolls made by different companies. $25.00 – $35.00 each.

TALKING VIEW-MASTER #AVB567, GAF, 1972. $20.00 – $25.00.

THE PARTRIDGE FAMILY

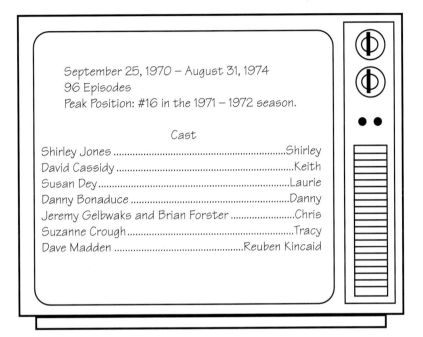

September 25, 1970 — August 31, 1974
96 Episodes
Peak Position: #16 in the 1971 — 1972 season.

Cast

Shirley Jones ....Shirley
David Cassidy ....Keith
Susan Dey..Laurie
Danny Bonaduce ....Danny
Jeremy Gelbwaks and Brian Forster ....Chris
Suzanne Crough..Tracy
Dave Madden ....Reuben Kincaid

Above and right: BOARD GAME, Milton Bradley, 1971.
$20.00 – $25.00.

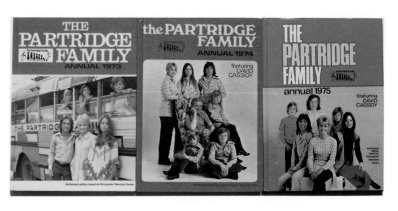

BRITISH ANNUALS, World, 1973 – 1975. $20.00 – $25.00 each.

BOOKLET, *Boys, Beauty and Popularity*, Tiger Beat, 1970s. By Susan Dey as told to Rochelle Reed. $15.00 – $20.00.

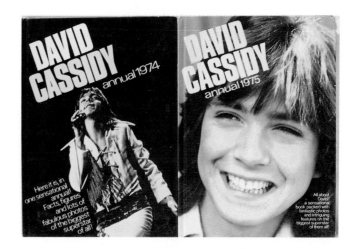

BRITISH ANNUALS, David Cassidy, World, 1974 – 1975. $20.00 – $25.00 each.

BUS, Remco, 1973. Box has illustration of garage on back and sides for storage and play. $300.00 – $500.00.

CLOCK FACE, Timesetters, 1972. Sold to put over an existing clock. Did not include hands or mechanism. $50.00 – $75.00.

CLOTHING LINE, Kate Greenaway, 1970s. Front and back of original tag pictured. Patches and stickers were attached to clothing that included jeans, tops, jackets, and jumpsuits. $50.00 – $75.00 each article.

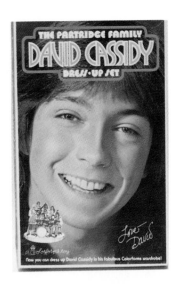

COLORFORMS, David Cassidy
Dress-Up Set, Colorforms, 1972.
$25.00 – $35.00.

COLORING BOOK #3839,
Saalfield, 1971.
$20.00 – $25.00.

COLORING BOOK #5399,
Artcraft, 1970.
$20.00 – $25.00.

COLORING BOOK #3997, Saalfield, 1971.
$20.00 – $25.00.

COMIC BOOKS, #1 – 9, Charlton, 1971 – 1972. Two different covers of #1 exist.
One with a black and white photo and one with a color photo. $10.00 – $15.00 each.

COMIC BOOKS, #1 0–18, Charlton, 1972 – 1973. $10.00 – $15.00 each.

COMIC BOOKS, #19 – 21, Charlton, 1973. $10.00 – $15.00 each.

COMIC BOOKS, David Cassidy, #1 – 6, Charlton, 1972. $10.00 – $15.00 each.

COMIC BOOKS, David Cassidy, #7 – 14, Charlton, 1972 – 1973. $10.00 – $15.00 each.

DAVID CASSIDY LOVER'S KIT, 16 Magazine, 1971. Includes lover's membership card, life-size portrait, maxi-poster pin-up, love message, and wallet photos. $30.00 – $40.00.

GUITAR, David Cassidy, Carnival Toys, 1970s. $75.00 – $100.00.

DOLL, Laurie Partridge, Remco, 1973. Color poster of David and Susan included in box. $150.00 – $200.00.

DOLL, Patti Partridge, Ideal, 1971. $100.00 – $150.00.

FAN CLUB KIT, Tiger Beat, 1971. Includes booklet, decoder, stickers, black flexible record, membership card, wallet photos, and mini poster. $50.00 – $75.00.

JIGSAW PUZZLE, David Cassidy, APC, 1972. $35.00 – $45.00.

JIGSAW PUZZLE, David Cassidy, APC, 1973. Life-size. Each piece is nearly six inches in diameter. $50.00 – $75.00.

LUNCH BOX, K.S.T., 1971. Metal box with metal or plastic thermos. $50.00 – $75.00 box.　　$20.00 – $25.00 metal thermos. $15.00 – $20.00 plastic thermos, 1973.

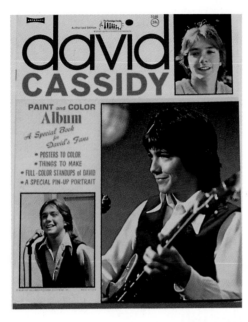

PAINT AND COLOR ALBUM, David, Artcraft, 1971. $25.00 – $35.00.

PAPER DOLL BOOKLET #4218, Susan Dey as Laurie, Artcraft, 1971. $25.00 – $35.00.

PAPER DOLL BOOKLET #5137, Artcraft, 1971. Two different versions. One with Jeremy Gelbwaks (1st Chris) and one with Brian Forster (2nd Chris). $25.00 – $35.00 each.

PAPER DOLL BOOKLET #4261, Susan Dey as Laurie, Artcraft, 1973. $25.00 – $35.00.

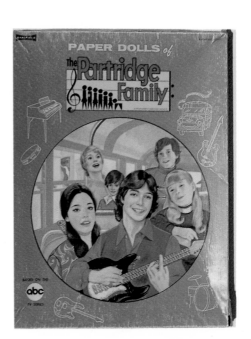

PAPER DOLL BOOKLET #5143, Artcraft, 1972.
$25.00 – $35.00.

PAPER DOLL BOX #6079,
Susan Dey as Laurie, Saalfield, 1973.
$35.00 – $45.00.

PAPER DOLL BOX #6050, Saalfield, 1971.
$35.00 – $45.00.

PAPER DOLL BOX #6050, Saalfield, 1972.
$35.00 – $45.00.

PAPER DOLL BOX #6157, Saalfield, 1972.
$35.00 – $45.00.

PAPER DOLL BOX #6050,
Saalfield, 1973.
$35.00 – $45.00.

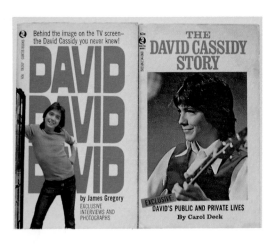

PAPERBACK BOOKS, *David, David, David* and *The David Cassidy Story*, Curtis Books, 1972. Two different covers of *The David Cassidy Story* exist. $5.00 – $8.00 each.

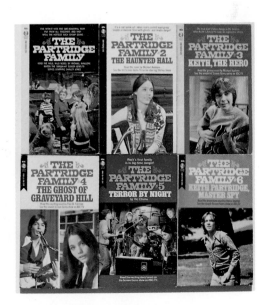

Above and right: PAPERBACK BOOKS, #1 – 17, Curtis Books, 1970 – 1973.
$3.00 – $5.00 each #1 – 9.
$5.00 – $8.00 each #10 – 17.

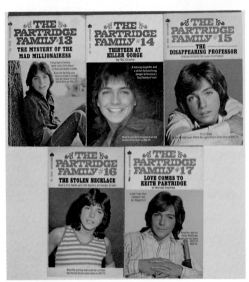

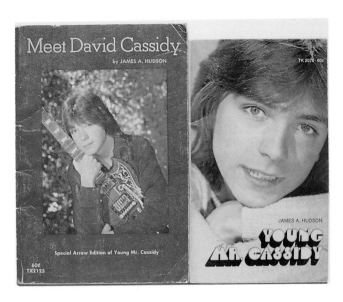

PAPERBACK BOOKS, *Meet David Cassidy* and *Young Mr. Cassidy*, Scholastic Books, 1972. $5.00 – $8.00 each.

PICTORIAL ACTIVITY ALBUM, Artcraft, 1973. $25.00 – $35.00.

PIN-ON BUTTON FAMILY TREE, Merry Motion, 1971. $100.00 – $125.00.

PIN-ON BUTTONS, Merry Motion, 1971. Set of six different. Tracy pictured. $20.00 – $25.00 each.

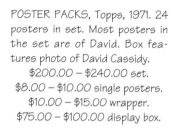

POSTER PACKS, Topps, 1971. 24 posters in set. Most posters in the set are of David. Box features photo of David Cassidy.
$200.00 – $240.00 set.
$8.00 – $10.00 single posters.
$10.00 – $15.00 wrapper.
$75.00 – $100.00 display box.

POSTER, David, Columbia Pictures, 1976. 12" x 18".
$8.00 – $12.00.

RADIO, 1970s. Cover is removable to insert any picture. Comes with chain to be worn as a necklace.
$100.00 – $150.00.

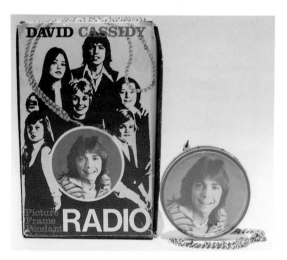

PURSE, Kate Greenaway 1970s. David's silhouette and signature along with the caption "I Think I Love You." Came in different colors.
$50.00 – $75.00.

RECORD/LP, "The Partridge Family Album," Bell, 1970. With photo insert.
$10.00 – $15.00.

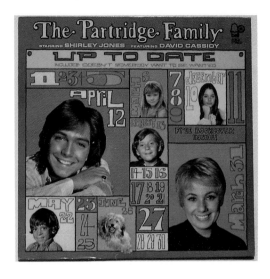

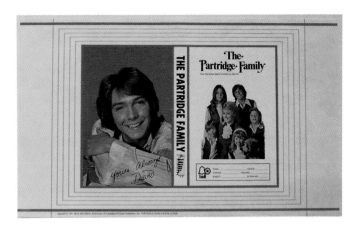

Left and above: RECORD/LP, "Up to Date," Bell, 1971. With bookcover.
$20.00 – $25.00.

RECORD/LP, "Christmas Card," Bell, 1971. With real, removable card or printed card cover. $20.00 – $25.00 each.

RECORD/LP, "Sound Magazine," Bell, 1971.
$5.00 – $10.00.

RECORD/LP, "Shopping Bag," Bell, 1972. With Partridge Family shopping bag. $20.00 – $25.00.

RECORD/LP, "At Home With Their Greatest Hits,"
Bell, 1972. $10.00 – $15.00.

RECORD/LP, "Notebook," Bell, 1972.
$10.00 – $15.00.

RECORD/LP, "Crossword Puzzle," Bell, 1973. Inside sleeve shows
answers to puzzle. $15.00 – $20.00.

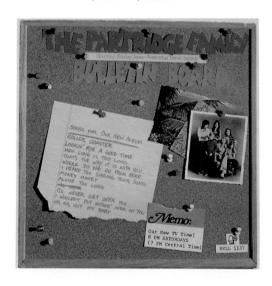

RECORD/LP, "Bulletin Board," Bell, 1973.
$15.00 – $20.00.

Left: RECORD/LP,
"World of the Partridge
Family," Bell, 1974. 2-LP
set of greatest hits.
$30.00 – $35.00.

Right: RECORD/LP, "The
Partridge Family," Lau-
rie House, 1970s. 2-LP
set of greatest hits.
Television mail-order
only. $30.00 – $35.00.

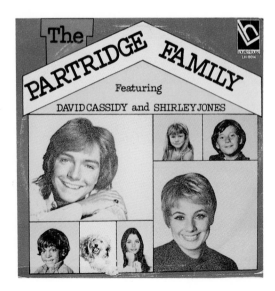

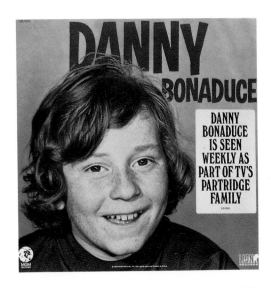

RECORDS, Bell, 1970s. Several different import LP's and 45's. "Greatest Hits" LP from Germany and "I Woke Up In Love This Morning"/"Twenty Four Hours a Day" 45 from Japan pictured.
$15.00 – $25.00 45's. $25.00 – $50.00 LP's.

RECORD/LP, "Danny Bonaduce," Lion Records, 1973.
$15.00 – $20.00.

RECORD/LP, "Ricky Segall and the Segalls," Bell, 1973. Sings selections from the television show. $10.00 – $15.00.

RECORD/45, "Dreamland"/"Blueberry You," Lion Records, 1973. Vocals by Danny Bonaduce.
$10.00 – $15.00.

RECORDS/45's, Bell, 1970 – 1971. "I Think I Love You"/"Somebody Wants to Love You"; "Doesn't Somebody Want to be Wanted?"/"You are Always on My Mind."
$10.00 – $15.00 each.

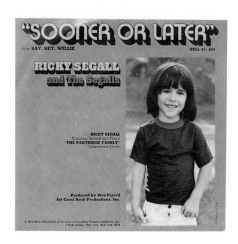

RECORD/45, "Sooner or Later"/"Say Hey, Willie,"
Bell, 1974. Vocals by Ricky Segall. $8.00 – $12.00.

SHEET MUSIC, Columbia, 1970 – 1973. Several different. "I Think I Love
You" and "It's One of Those Nights (Yes Love)" pictured.
$10.00 – $15.00 each.

TALKING VIEW-MASTER,
Money Manager, GAF, 1971.
$25.00 – $35.00.

SONG BOOKS, Columbia, 1970 – 1973. Several different. Shopping Bag song book pictured. Inside
contains several pictures and a story about the
cast and show. $20.00 – $25.00 each.

SPIRAL NOTEBOOK,
David, Westab, 1972.
$10.00 – $15.00.

THREE RING BINDER, David, Westab,
1972. $15.00 – $20.00.

TRADING CARD SET #1, O-Pee-Chee, 1971. 55 yellow cards in set. Puzzle
and song backs. O-Pee-Chee cards were made in Canada under license
from Topps and are the same as the U.S. Topps set.
$50.00 – $75.00 set. $1.00 – $1.25 single cards.
$10.00 – $15.00 wrapper. $60.00 – $75.00 display box.

TRADING CARD SET #2, Topps, 1971. 55 blue cards in set.
Puzzle and song backs. Topps sets include three different
display boxes similar to the one pictured in set #1. The first
one is a half-size box with a 5¢ price and the other two are
full-size, one with a 5¢ price and the other a 10¢ price.
$50.00 – $75.00 set. $1.00 – $1.25 single cards.
$10.00 – $15.00 wrapper. $60.00 – $75.00 display box.

TV GUIDES, 1970 – 1972.
10/17/70 Cast; 05/22/71 David; 12/18/71 Cast;
07/18/72 David.
$10.00 – $15.00 each.

TRADING CARD SET #3, Topps, 1971. 88 green cards in
set. Puzzle and song backs.
$150.00 – $175.00 set. $1.75 – $2.00 single cards.
$10.00 – $15.00 wrapper. $60.00 – $75.00 display box.

VIEW-MASTER #B569, Money Manager, GAF, 1971. Titled and untitled versions exist. $20.00 – $25.00.

VIEW-MASTER #B592, Male Chauvinist, GAF, 1973. $20.00 – $25.00.

Other items not pictured:

3-D PHOTOS, David Cassidy and Partridge Family, Merry Motion, 1971. 11" x 14" full-color photos. $35.00 – $40.00 each.

BEACH TOWEL, David Cassidy, HI-C, 1970s. $40.00 – $50.00.

BOOKLETS, Tiger Beat, 1970s. 1001 Secret Facts About the Partridge Family; David's Private Photo Album; Partridge Family Fun Album; Dynamic David Cassidy; Life, Love and David by Shirley Jones; Susan Dey's Private Journal; The Secret of David Cassidy. $15.00 – $20.00 each.

BULLETIN BOARD, 1970s. 18" x 24" red cork board with the Partridge Family logo music staff in white at top. $50.00 – $75.00.

CLOCK FACE, David, Timesetters, 1972. Sold to put over an existing clock. Did not include hands or mechanism. $50.00 – $75.00.

COLORING BOOK, Saalfield, 1970. Photo cover of entire family standing in front of bus. $20.00 – $25.00.

DAVID CASSIDY MAIL-A-WAY ITEMS, Tiger Beat, 1970s. Different items to send for including Love Charms, Super Luv Stickers, and Choker Luv Beads. $15.00 – $20.00 each.

DAVID CASSIDY STICK-UP, Personality Prints, 1970s. Photo of David in clear package and header card. $20.00 – $25.00.

FAN CLUB KIT, Tiger Beat, 1972. Includes booklet, pink photo cardboard record, wallet photos, poster, membership card, stickers, and David pin-up. $50.00 – $75.00.

FAN CLUB KIT, David Cassidy, Tiger Beat, 1972. Includes calendar poster, blue photo cardboard record, membership card, stickers, decoder, and autographed photo. $50.00 – $75.00.

FUN BOOK, 1970s. Photo of family on cover. Inside are activities which include coloring. $25.00 – $35.00.

GUITAR, David, Carnival Toys, 1970s. Larger red version with same photo and signature as smaller guitar with additional caption, "I Think I Love You." $100.00 – $125.00.

JEWELRY, 1970s. Bracelets and necklaces with Partridge Family tags. $35.00 – $45.00 each.

PAPERBACK BOOK, *For Girls Only*, Tiger Beat, 1971. By Susan Dey. $10.00 – $15.00.

PAPERBACK BOOK, *Cooking, Cleaning, and Falling in Love*, Tiger Beat, 1973. By Susan Dey. $10.00 – 15.00.

PAPER DOLL BOX #6024. Susan Dey as Laurie, Saalfield, 1972. Flat square box that features two photos. One of Susan Dey and the other the entire family. $35.00 – $45.00.

PAPER DOLL BOX, Saalfield, 1971. Boxed version of booklet #5137. $35.00 – $45.00.

RECORD/45, "I'll Be Your Magician"/"Fortune Lady," Lion Records, 1973. Vocals by Danny Bonaduce. Without picture sleeve. $5.00 – $8.00.

RECORDS/45's, Bell, 1971 – 1973. "I'll Meet You Halfway"/"Morning Rider on the Road"; "I Woke Up in Love This Morning"/"Twenty Four Hours a Day"; "It's One of Those Nights"/"One Night Stand"; "Am I Losing You"/"If You Ever Go"; "Breaking Up is Hard to Do"/"I'm Here, You're Here"; "Looking Through the Eyes of Love"/"Storybook Love"; "Friend and a Lover"/"Something's Wrong"; "Lookin' For a Good Time"/"Money, Money." Without picture sleeves. $3.00 – $5.00 each.

RECORD CASE, 1970s. 25" x 22" red box with white front and colorful Partridge Family logo music staff. $150.00 – $200.00.

SLIDE PUZZLE, David Cassidy, 1970s. $25.00 – $35.00.

T-SHIRTS, 1970s. Various styles, including large color face of David. $20.00 – $25.00 each.

TRADING CARDS, Scanlens, 1970s. Issued in Australia under license from Topps. Set of 55. $110.00 – $165.00 set; $2.00 – $3.00 single cards; $10.00 – $15.00 wrapper; $75.00 – $100.00 display box.

WRISTWATCH, 1970s. Working watch with family photo on face. $150.00 – $200.00.

THE PATTY DUKE SHOW

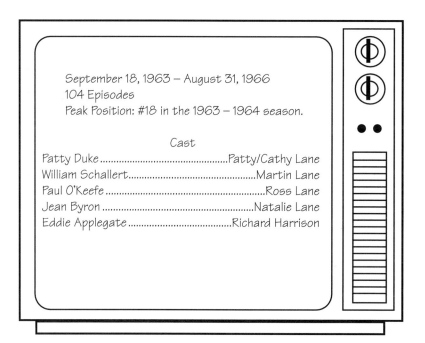

September 18, 1963 – August 31, 1966
104 Episodes
Peak Position: #18 in the 1963 – 1964 season.

Cast

Patty Duke..Patty/Cathy Lane
William Schallert...Martin Lane
Paul O'Keefe...Ross Lane
Jean Byron..Natalie Lane
Eddie Applegate..Richard Harrison

Above and right: BOARD GAME, Milton Bradley, 1963.
$30.00 – $40.00.

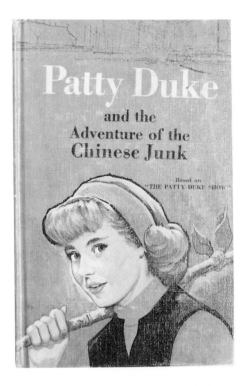

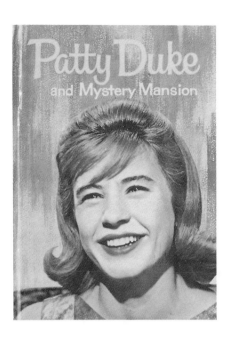

BOOK, *Patty Duke and the Adventure of the Chinese Junk*, Whitman, 1966. $8.00 – $10.00.

BOOK, *Patty Duke and Mystery Mansion*, Whitman, 1964. $8.00 – $10.00.

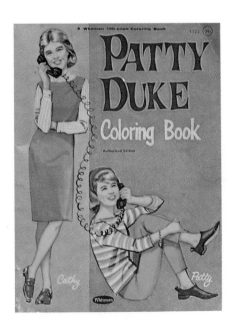

COLORING BOOK #1122, Whitman, 1964. $20.00 – $25.00.

COLORING BOOK #1141, Whitman, 1966. $20.00 – $25.00.

JIGSAW PUZZLE, Whitman, 1963.
$25.00 – $35.00.

PAPER DOLL BOOKLET #1991, Whitman, 1963.
$25.00 – $30.00.

PAPERBACK BOOK, *Patty Goes to Washington*, Ace Books, 1964.
$10.00 – $15.00.

PAPER DOLL BOOKLET #1991, Whitman,
1964. $25.00 – $30.00.

PAPER DOLL BOX, Whitman, 1963. Includes Patty and Cathy dolls.
$35.00 – $40.00.

RECORD/LP, "Don't Just Stand There," United Artists, 1965. $20.00 – $25.00.

RECORD/LP, "Patty," United Artists, 1966. $20.00 – $25.00.

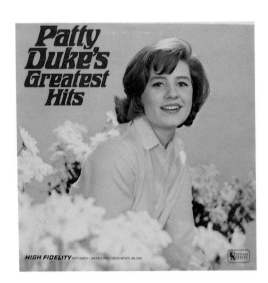

RECORD/LP, "Patty Duke's Greatest Hits," United Artists, 1966. $20.00 – $25.00.

RECORD/LP, "TV's Teen Star," United Artists, 1967. $20.00 – $25.00.

TV GUIDES, 1963 – 1964.
12/28/63 Duke (pictured); 08/29/64 Duke,
Schallert, and Lane.
$8.00 – $12.00 each.

Other items not pictured:

ASHTRAY, 1960s. Square-shaped ashtray in photo cover box. $30.00 – $40.00.

CHARM JEWELRY SET, Standard Toykraft, 1963. Photo cover window box. Includes jewelry box and small charms. $50.00 – $75.00.

CHEERLEADER LUSTER KIT, 1965. In photo cover box. $40.00 – $50.00.

DOLL, Patty Duke, Horseman, 1963. 12" doll comes with telephone and photo of Patty Duke. $200.00 – $250.00.

GLAMOUR SET, Standard Toykraft, 1963. Photo cover on window box. Includes plastic mirror, brush, and comb. $50.00 – $75.00.

LEATHER ACCESSORIES KIT, 1965. In photo cover box. $40.00 – $50.00.

PAPER DOLL BOX #4609, Patty Duke Fashion Wardrobe, Whitman, 1965. $35.00 – $40.00.

PAPER DOLL BOX #4775, Whitman, 1965. Includes Patty and Cathy dolls. $35.00 – $40.00.

RECORDS/45's, United Artists, 1965. "Don't Just Stand There"/"Everything But Love"; "Say Something Funny"/"Funny Little Butterflies." Vocals by Patty Duke. With picture sleeves. $10.00 – $15.00 each.

RECORDS/45's, United Artists, 1965 – 1967. "Whenever She Holds You"/"Nothing But Love"; "The World Is Watching Us"/"Little Things Mean Alot"; "Why Don't They Understand"/"Danke Schoen"; "And Were We Strangers"/"Dona, Dona"; "The Wall Came Tumbling Down"/"What Makes You Special." Vocals by Patty Duke. Without picture sleeves. $5.00 – $10.00 each.

SIGMUND AND THE SEA MONSTERS

September 8, 1973 – October 18, 1975
29 Episodes

Cast

Johnny Whitaker...Johnny Stuart
Billy Barty ....Sigmund
Scott Kolden...Scott Stuart
Mary Wickes... Zelda Marshall
Rip Taylor..Sheldon the Sea Genie

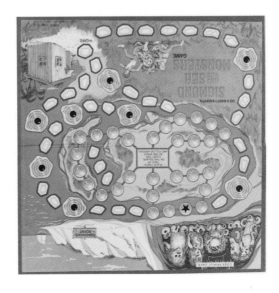

Above and right: BOARD GAME, Milton Bradley, 1975.
$20.00 – $25.00.

Left: RECORD/LP, "Friends - Music from Sigmund and the Sea Monsters," Chelsea Records, 1973. Vocals by Johnny Whitaker.
$20.00 – $25.00.

RECORD/45, "Friends"/"You You," Chelsea Records, 1973. Vocals by Johnny Whitaker.
$10.00 – $15.00.

Left: COLORING BOOK #C1853, Saalfield, 1974.
$15.00 – $20.00.

VIEW-MASTER #B595, GAF, 1974.
$20.00 – $25.00.

LUNCH BOX, Aladdin, 1974. Metal box with plastic thermos.
$40.00 – $50.00 box. $15.00 – $20.00 thermos.

Other items not pictured:

COLORING BOOK #4634, Artcraft, 1974. Illustration of Johnny and Sigmund on the beach, 39¢ cover. $15.00 – $20.00.

COLORING BOOK #C0945, Saalfield, 1974. Same illustration as #4634, but with a 29¢ cover. $15.00 – $20.00.

HALLOWEEN COSTUME, Sigmund, Ben Cooper, 1970s. $40.00 – $60.00.

TALKING VIEW-MASTER #AVB595, GAF, 1974. $25.00 – $30.00.

THE SIX MILLION DOLLAR MAN

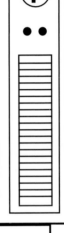

October 20, 1973 – February 27, 1978
104 Episodes
Peak Position: #9 in the 1975 – 1977 seasons.

Cast
Lee Majors...Steve Austin
Richard Anderson......................................Oscar Goldman
Alan Oppenheimer/Martin E. Brooks............Dr. Rudy Wells
Jennifer Darling...Peggy Callahan

ACTIVITY BOOK #C2471, Rand McNally, 1977.
$8.00 – $10.00.

BIONIC TATTOOS AND STICKERS, Kenner,
1976. $8.00 – $12.00.

BIONIC TRANSPORT & REPAIR STA-
TION, Kenner, 1975. $25.00 – $35.00.

Above and right: BOARD GAME, Parker Brothers, 1975.
$10.00 – $15.00.

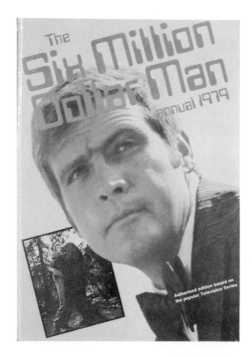

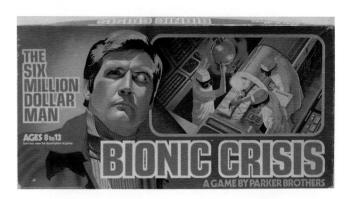

CARD GAME, Bionic Crisis, Parker Brothers, 1976. $10.00 – $15.00.

BRITISH ANNUALS, Stafford Pemberton, 1977 –
1979. 1979 annual shown. $10.00 – $15.00 each.

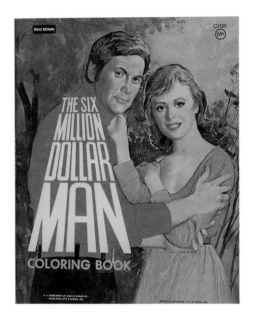

COLORING BOOK #C1520, Rand McNally, 1977.
$8.00 – $10.00.

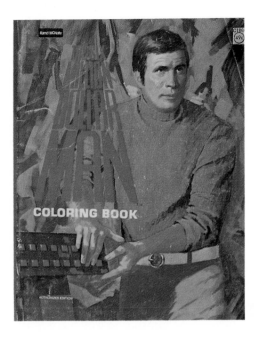

COLORING BOOK #C1868, Rand McNally, 1976.
$8.00 – $10.00.

Left and below: COMIC BOOK MAGAZINES, #1 – 7,
Charlton, 1976. $3.00 – $5.00 each.

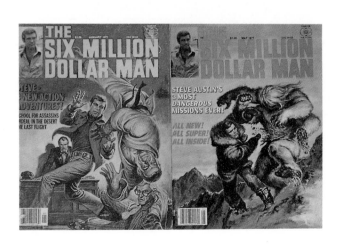

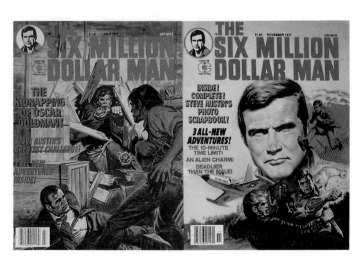

COMIC BOOKS, #1 – 9, Charlton, 1976 – 1978. $3.00 – $5.00 each.

Left: JIGSAW PUZZLES, APC, 1976 – 1977. Several different. #1536 pictured. $8.00 – $12.00 each.

Right: DOLLS, Oscar Goldman and Steve Austin, Kenner, 1975 – 1977. Oscar doll (1977) in original box comes with an exploding briefcase. Steve with bionic grip (1975) pictured. $35.00 – $45.00 each.

DOLL OUTFIT, O.S.I. Undercover Assignment, Kenner, 1976. $10.00 – $15.00.

HALLOWEEN COSTUME, Steve Austin, Ben Cooper, 1974. Blue or red body suit. $10.00 – $15.00.

Left: CUP AND TUMBLER, Dawn, 1976. $8.00 – $10.00 each.

Right: JIGSAW PUZZLES #1240-1243, APC, 1975. 4 different in canisters. #1242 pictured. $8.00 – $12.00 each.

LUNCH BOX, Aladdin, 1974. Metal box with plastic thermos.
$20.00 – $25.00 box. $8.00 – $12.00 thermos.

O.S.I. HEADQUARTERS, Kenner, 1976. Play-set for 12" dolls. $40.00 – $60.00.

LUNCH BOX, Aladdin, 1978. Metal box with plastic thermos.
$20.00 – $25.00 box. $8.00 – $12.00 thermos.

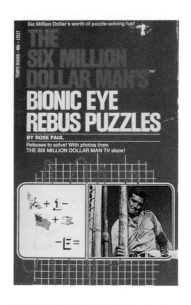

PAPERBACK BOOK, *Bionic Eye Rebus Puzzles*, Tempo Books, 1976. $3.00 – $5.00.

PAPERBACK BOOKS, *Cyborg #1* and *Cyborg #2*, Warner, 1972 – 1973. Two different covers for *Cyborg #1*. $3.00 – $5.00 each.

PAPERBACK BOOKS, #1 – 6, Warner Books, 1975.
$3.00 – $5.00 each.

PAPERBACK BOOKS, *The Secret of Bigfoot Pass*, Berkely, 1976 and *The Six Million Dollar Man and the Bionic Woman*, Scholastic Books, 1976. $3.00 – $5.00 each.

POSTER PUT-ON, Bi-Rite, 1978.
$5.00 – $8.00.

RAINCOAT, Universal, 1976. Back has illustration of Steve Austin running. $30.00 – $35.00.

RECORDS, Peter Pan, 1975 – 1978. Several different 45's and LP's with adventure stories. Some include story books. LP "Christmas Adventures" and 45 "Elves Revolt" pictured. $5.00 – $8.00 each.

TALKING VIEW-MASTER #AVB559, GAF, 1974.
$15.00 – $20.00.

TRADING CARDS, Donruss, 1975. 66 stickers in set with puzzle backs.
$40.00 – $60.00 set. $.50 – $1.00 single stickers.
$3.00 – $5.00 wrapper. $20.00 – $25.00 display box.

TRADING CARDS, Topps, 1975. 55 cards in set. Import from Mexico. Same as U.S. test set.
$200.00 – $275.00 set. $3.00 – $5.00 single cards.
$8.00 – $12.00 wrapper. $20.00 – $25.00 display box.

TRADING CARDS, Monty, 1975. Import set of 72 with puzzle backs. Cards are unnumbered from Holland.
$75.00 – $100.00 set. $1.00 – $1.50 single cards.
$5.00 – $8.00 wrapper. $15.00 – $20.00 display box.

TV GUIDES, 1974 – 1976.
05/18/74 Majors illustrated;
08/28/76 Majors illustrated.
$3.00 – $5.00 each.

TRASH CAN, Cheinco, 1976.
$25.00 – $30.00.

VIEW-MASTER #B559, GAF, 1974.
$10.00 – $15.00.

Other items not pictured:

WRISTWATCH, Universal,
1976. $50.00 – $75.00.

BACKPACK RADIO, Kenner, 1970s. In box. $20.00 – $25.00.

BANK, Animals Plus, 1976. 12" plastic figural. $10.00 – $15.00.

BATHROBE, 1970s. $20.00 – $30.00.

BIONIC ACTION CLUB KIT, Kenner, 1973. Mail-away with stickers, photos, card, autograph, and button. $30.00 – $40.00.

BIONIC CYCLE, Kenner, 1973. $20.00 – $25.00.

C.B. RADIO HEADSET RECEIVER, Kenner, 1970. $20.00 – $25.00.

COLORING BOOK #C1832, Artcraft, 1974. Illustration of Steve on beach. $8.00 – $10.00.

COMMAND CONSOLE, Kenner, 1976. $35.00 – $45.00.

CRITICAL ASSIGNMENT-ARMS, Kenner, 1976. $15.00 – $20.00.

CRITICAL ASSIGNMENT-LEGS, Kenner, 1976. $15.00 – $20.00.

DIP DOTS PAINT BY NUMBER SET, Kenner, 1970s. $10.00 – $15.00.

DOLL, Bigfoot, Kenner, 1978. $40.00 – $50.00.

DOLL, Maskatron, Kenner, 1970s. $40.00 – $50.00.

DOLL, Steve Austin, Kenner, 1975. With biosonic arm. $35.00 – $45.00.

DOLL OUTFITS, Adventure Test Flight at 75,000 Feet and Mission to Mars Adventure Set, Kenner, 1976. $10.00 – $15.00 each.

DOODLE ART SET, 1970s. Art set in tube. $15.00 – $20.00.

FRAME TRAY PUZZLE, 1976. $10.00 – $15.00.

GIVE-A-SHOW PROJECTOR, Kenner, 1975. $20.00 – $25.00.

LAUNCH DRAG SET, Kenner, 1976. $25.00 – $35.00.

MISSION CONTROL CENTER, Kenner, 1970s. $35.00 – $45.00.

MISSION VEHICLE, Kenner, 1976. $30.00 – $40.00.

MODEL KITS, MPC, 1975. Bionic Bustout; Evil Rider Motorcycle; Fight for Survival; Jaws of Doom. $20.00 – $25.00 each.

MOVIE VIEWER, Kenner, 1975. Hand-held viewer for movie cassettes. $25.00 – $30.00.

MOVIE VIEWER CASSETTES, Kenner, 1975. Several different in numbered boxes sold separately for movie viewer. $10.00 – $15.00 each.

PLAY-DOH ACTION SET, Kenner, 1977. $10.00 – $15.00.

PLAYSUIT, 1970s. Australian child-size suit on card. $25.00 – $30.00.

PORTA-COMMUNICATOR, Kenner, 1978. $15.00 – $20.00.

SEE-A-SHOW VIEWER, Kenner, 1970s. On card with illustration of Steve Austin. $8.00 – $12.00.

SLIDE PROJECTOR SET, Chad Bally, 1976. Illustration of Steve Austin on box. Inside has a 9" slide projector and 16 filmstrips. $25.00 – $30.00.

TURBO TOWER OF POWER AND CYCLE SET, Kenner, 1976. $35.00 – $45.00.

VENUS SPACE PROBE, Kenner, 1976. $35.00 – $45.00.

WRISTWATCH, MZ Berger, 1970s. Illustration of Steve running in red outfit. $50.00 – $75.00.

STARSKY AND HUTCH

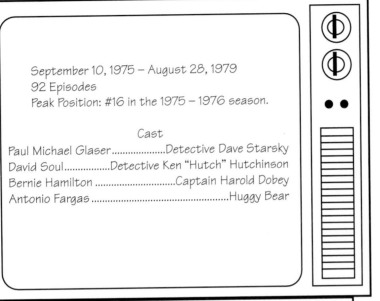

September 10, 1975 – August 28, 1979
92 Episodes
Peak Position: #16 in the 1975 – 1976 season.

Cast
Paul Michael Glaser....................Detective Dave Starsky
David Soul................Detective Ken "Hutch" Hutchinson
Bernie Hamilton ....Captain Harold Dobey
Antonio Fargas ....Huggy Bear

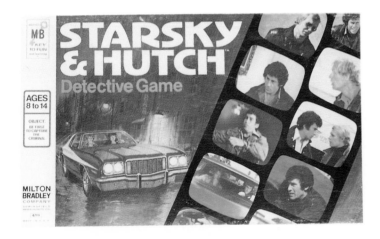

Above and right: BOARD GAME, Milton Bradley, 1976.
$20.00 – $25.00.

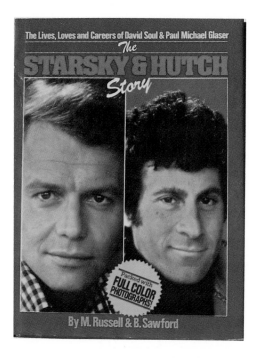

BOOK, *The Starsky and Hutch Story*, Castle Books, 1977. Hardback book. $10.00 – $15.00.

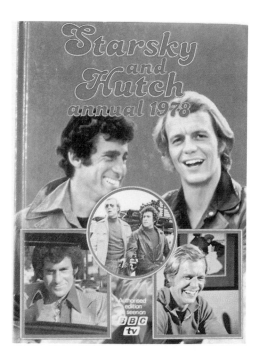

BRITISH ANNUALS, 1978 – 1981. 1978 annual pictured. $15.00 – $20.00 each.

DOLLS, Starsky, Hutch, Captain Dobey, Chopper, and Huggy Bear, Mego, 1976. Starsky and Hutch dolls pictured. $20.00 – $25.00 each.

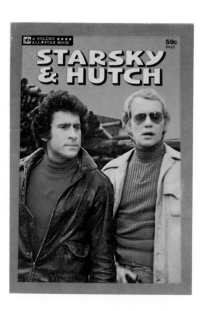

GOLDEN ALL-STAR BOOKS, Golden Press, 1977 Two different. #6423 pictured. $8.00 – $10.00 each.

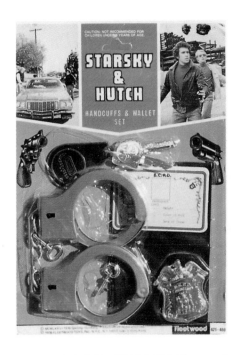

JIGSAW PUZZLES, HG Toys, 1976. Several different. #492-05 and 492-06 pictured. $8.00 – $12.00 each.

HANDCUFFS AND WALLET SET, Fleetwood, 1976. $20.00 – 25.00.

POSTER PUT-ON, Bi-Rite, 1976. $5.00 – $8.00.

PAPERBACK BOOKS, #1 – 8, Ballantine Books, 1975 – 1978. $3.00 – $5.00 each.

SHOOT-OUT TARGET SET, Berwick, 1977. European.
$50.00 – 75.00.

RADIO-CONTROLLED CAR, Galoob, 1977.
$30.00 – $45.00.

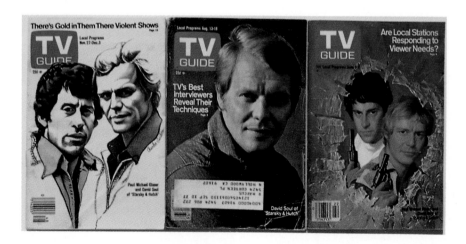

TV GUIDES, 1975 – 1978.
11/15/75 Soul and Glaser (not pictured); 11/27/76 Soul and Glaser illustrated; 08/13/77
Soul; 06/03/78 Soul and Glaser illustrated.
$5.00 – $8.00 each.

Other items not pictured:

CAP FIRING GUN SET, Lone Star, 1970s. Die-cast gun in box with photo cover. $75.00 – $100.00.

CORGI GRAN TORINO, Mettoy, 1976. $35.00 – $45.00.

CORGI JR. GRAN TORINO, Mettoy, 1976. $20.00 – $25.00.

DASHBOARD SET, 1976. $35.00 – $45.00.

FIGURES, Starsky and Hutch, Palitoy, 1977. Figures in illustrated box. $45.00 – $60.00.

GRAN TORINO, Mego, 1976. For 8" dolls. $50.00 – $75.00.

GUN, 9MM Automatic Water Pistol, Fleetwood, 1976. $20.00 – $25.00.

GUN, Die-Cast Metal Revolver, Lone Star, 1970s. Gun with holster. $75.00 – $100.00.

GUN, .357 Magnum Water Pistol, Fleetwood, 1976. $20.00 – $25.00.

HALLOWEEN COSTUMES, Starsky and Hutch, Ben Cooper, 1976. $20.00 – $25.00 each.

IRON-ONS, 1970s. Several different styles. $5.00 – $8.00 each.

PINBACK BADGE, 1977. Badge on card. $8.00 – $12.00.

POSTERS, 1970s. Several styles, including a collage. $10.00 – $15.00 each.

RECORD/45, "Starsky and Hutch Theme"/"Charlie's Angels Theme," United Artists, 1976. Original theme for the television show. Instrumentals by The Ventures. $8.00 – $12.00.

REPEATER CAP GUN, Fleetwood, 1976. $15.00 – $20.00.

T-SHIRTS, 1970s. Several different styles. $8.00 – $12.00 each.

TARGET SET, Placo Toys, 1977. $40.00 – $50.00.

TARGET RANGE GAME, Arco, 1977. Boxed set with photo cover. $50.00 – $75.00.

TRADING CARDS, Monty, 1970s. 72 cards in unnumbered set. Import from Holland. Puzzle backs. $150.00 – $200.00 set; $2.00 – $3.00 single cards; $5.00 – $10.00 wrapper; $20.00 – $25.00 display box.

TV VIEWER, Fleetwood, 1976. Four rolls of photos with small plastic screen on card. $20.00 – $25.00.

WALKIE TALKIES, Mettoy, 1970s. Thin horizontal box that features color photo of Starsky and Hutch. $50.00 – $75.00.

THAT GIRL

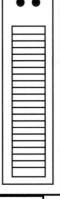

September 8, 1966 – September 10, 1971
135 Episodes
Peak Position: Not in the top 25.

Cast

Marlo Thomas ....Ann Marie
Ted Bessell...Don Hollinger

COLORING BOOK #9658, Artcraft, 1968.
$20.00 – $25.00.

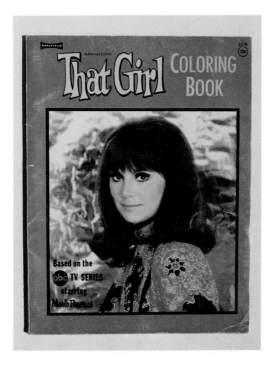

COLORING BOOK #4539, Saalfield, 1970.
$20.00 – $25.00.

PAPER DOLL BOOKLET #1379, Saalfield, 1967.
$25.00 – $35.00.

PAPERBACK BOOK, Popular
Library, 1971. $5.00 – $8.00.

TV GUIDES, 1966 – 1970.
11/12/66 Thomas; 12/02/67 Thomas
and Thomas; 03/17/69 Thomas;
08/08/70 Thomas and Bessell.
$8.00 – $10.00 each.

PAPER DOLL BOOKLET #1351, Saalfield, 1967.
$25.00 – $35.00.

Other items not pictured:

BOARD GAME, Remco, 1968. $75.00 – $100.00.

COLORING BOOK #4513, Saalfield, 1967. Illustration of Ann Marie with secretary in background. $20.00 – $25.00.

PAPER DOLL BOOKLET, Saalfield, 1967. Illustration of Ann Marie with color photo in window. $25.00 – $35.00.

WIG CASE, 1960s. "That Girl" written on front. $40.00 – $50.00.

THREE'S COMPANY

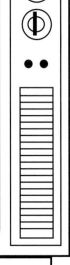

March 15, 1977 – September 18, 1984
164 Episodes
Peak Position: #2 in the 1978 – 1979 season.

Cast

John Ritter...Jack Tripper
Joyce DeWitt...Janet Wood
Suzanne Somers..Chrissy Snow
Norman Fell ....Stanley Roper
Audra Lindley..Helen Roper
Jenilee Harrison ....Cindy Snow
Priscilla Barnes..Terri Alden
Richard Kline..Larry Dallas
Don Knotts ....Ralph Furley

DOLL, Chrissy, Mego, 1978. $35.00 – $45.00.

JIGSAW PUZZLE, Chrissy, APC, 1978.
$10.00 – $15.00.

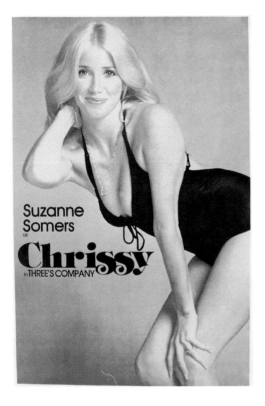

POSTER, Suzanne Somers as Chrissy, Dargis, 1977.
$10.00 – $15.00.

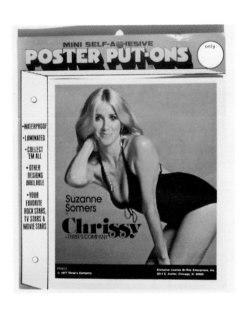

POSTER PUT-ON, Suzanne Somers as Chrissy,
Bi-Rite, 1977. $5.00 – $8.00.

TRADING CARDS, Topps, 1978. 44 stickers and 16 puzzle cards.
$8.00 – $12.00 set. $.10 – $.25 single stickers and cards.
$1.00 – $2.00 wrapper. $5.00 – $8.00 display box.

Other items not pictured:

SHEET MUSIC, Theme, 1979. Cast photo. $8.00 – $12.00.

TV GUIDES, 1978 – 1983.
05/20/78 Cast illustrated; 08/04/79 Joyce De Witt (not
pictured); 03/14/81 Suzanne Somers; 03/13/82 Cast;
11/20/82 Cast illustrated; 09/24/83 Cast illustrated.
$3.00 – $5.00 each.

THE WALTONS

September 14, 1972 – August 20, 1981
178 Episodes
Peak Position: #8 in the 1974 – 1975 season.

Cast

Ralph Waite...John Walton
Michael Learned ....Olivia Walton
Will Geer.....................................Zeb "Grandpa" Walton
Ellen Corby............................Esther "Grandma" Walton
Richard Thomas ....John-Boy
John Walmsley ....Jason
Judy Norton ....Mary Ellen
Eric Scott...Ben
Mary Elizabeth McDonough ....Erin
David S. Harper...Jim-Bob
Kami Cotler...Elizabeth

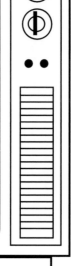

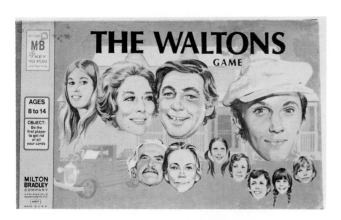

Above and right: BOARD GAME, Milton Bradley, 1975.
$10.00 – $15.00.

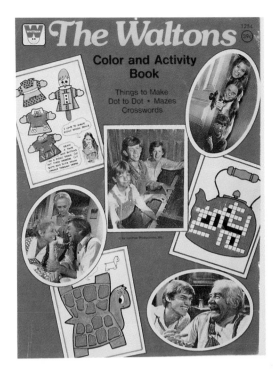

BOOKS, #1 – 6, Whitman, 1975. Set of hardback books.
$4.00 – $6.00 each.

COLORING AND ACTIVITY BOOK #1254, Whitman,
1975. $10.00 – $15.00.

LITTLE GOLDEN BOOK,
*The Waltons and the
Birthday Present*, Golden
Press, 1975.
$5.00 – $8.00.

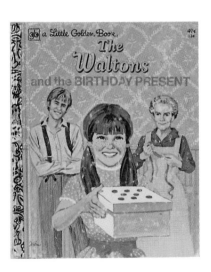

DOLLS, John Boy and Ellen, Mom and Pop, and
Grandma and Grandpa, Mego, 1974. 8" dolls sold
in pairs and single boxes.
$15.00 – $20.00 single in box.
$25.00 – $30.00 each pair in box.

FARMHOUSE, Mego, 1974. 38" x 26" boxed
playset for the 8" dolls. $50.00 – $75.00.

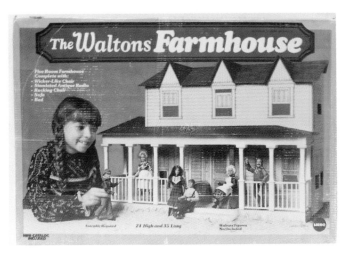

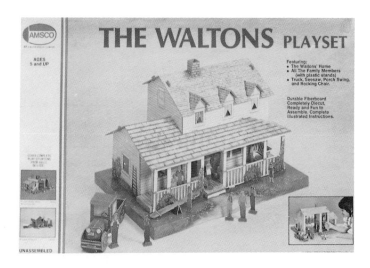

FARMHOUSE PLAYSET, Amsco, 1975. 20" x 14" boxed playset with cardboard figures. $30.00 – $40.00.

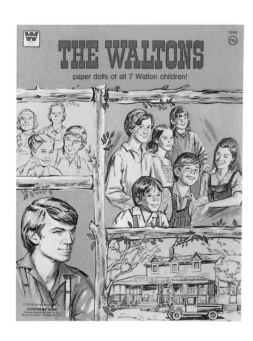

PAPER DOLL BOOKLET #1995, Whitman, 1975. $15.00 – $20.00.

LUNCH BOX, Aladdin, 1973. Metal box with plastic thermos. $30.00 – $40.00 box. $10.00 – $15.00 thermos.

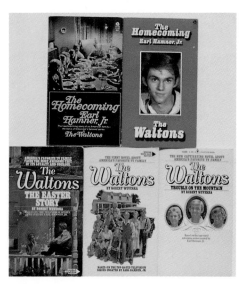

PAPERBACK BOOKS, *The Homecoming*, Avon, 1970, first printing; *The Homecoming*, Avon, 1970; *The Easter Story*, Bantam, 1976; *The Waltons*, Bantam, 1974; *Trouble on the Mountain*, Bantam, 1975. $3.00 – $5.00 each.

PAPER DOLL BOX #4334, Whitman, 1974. $20.00 – $25.00.

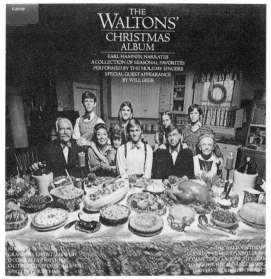

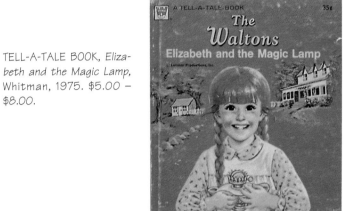

TELL-A-TALE BOOK, *Elizabeth and the Magic Lamp*, Whitman, 1975. $5.00 – $8.00.

RECORD/LP, "The Waltons' Christmas Album," Columbia, 1974. Vocals by The Holiday Singers. Narration by Earl Hamner with special guest appearance by Will Geer. $8.00 – $12.00.

TRUCK, Mego, 1975. For 8" dolls. $20.00 – $30.00.

TALKING VIEW-MASTER #AVB596, GAF, 1972. $15.00 – $20.00.

TV GUIDES, 1973 – 1977.
04/28/73 Cast illustrated; 04/13/74 Cast; 10/26/74 Waite, Thomas, and Geer illustrated; 08/23/75 Waite, Thomas, and Learned illustrated; 08/21/75 Thomas, Geer, Corby; 06/25/77 Cast illustrated. $3.00 – $5.00 each.

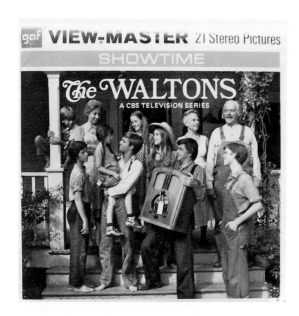

VIEW-MASTER #B596, GAF,
1972. $10.00 – $15.00.

Other items not pictured:

BARN PLAYSET, Mego, 1974. Playset for 8" dolls. $50.00 – $75.00.

COLORING BOOK #1028, Whitman, 1975. Photo cover. $10.00 – $15.00.

COOKBOOK, *The Waltons Family Cookbook*, 1970s. Paperback book. $10.00 – $15.00.

COUNTRY STORE PLAYSET, Mego, 1974. Playset for the 8" dolls. $50.00 – $75.00.

DIE-CAST METAL TRUCK, 1970s. On card with family photo. $15.00 – $20.00.

KITE FUN BOOK, Western Publishing, 1980. 5" x 7" comic book distributed by the electric company with comics, activities, and instructions for safe kite flying. $10.00 – $15.00.

RECORD/LP, "Joe Conely and Eric Scott of The Waltons," United National, 1979. $15.00 – $20.00.

SHEET MUSIC, Theme, 1973. Photo cover. $8.00 – $10.00.

STICKER BOOK, #1691, Whitman, 1975. $20.00 – $25.00.

TRADING CARDS, Topps, 1973. Test set of 50 photo cards with puzzle backs.
$2,000.00 – $2,500.00 set; $30.00 – $40.00 single cards; $125.00 – $150.00 wrapper.

WELCOME BACK KOTTER

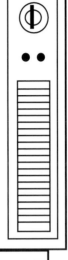

September 9, 1975 – August 3, 1979
98 Episodes
Peak Position: #13 in the 1976 – 77 season.

Cast

Gabriel Kaplan...Gabe Kotter
Marcia Strassman..Julie Kotter
John Travolta...Vinnie Barbarino
Robert Hegyes ....Juan Epstein
Ron Palillo..Arnold Horshack
Lawrence Hilton-Jacobs............Frederick "Boom Boom"
Washington
John Sylvester White ....Michael Woodman

BRUNCH BAG, Barbarino, Aladdin, 1977. Vinyl bag with plastic thermos.
$50.00 – $75.00 bag. $15.00 – $20.00 thermos.

CALCULATING WHEEL, Pamco, 1976.
$8.00 – $12.00.

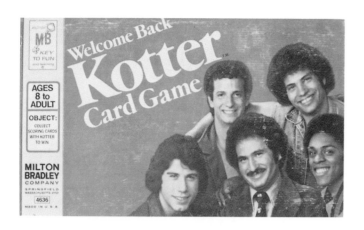

CARD GAME, Milton Bradley, 1976.
$10.00 – $15.00.

CLASSROOM PLAYSET, Mattel, 1976. Playset for 10" dolls.
Includes chalk, record, stickers, and furniture.
$45.00 – $55.00.

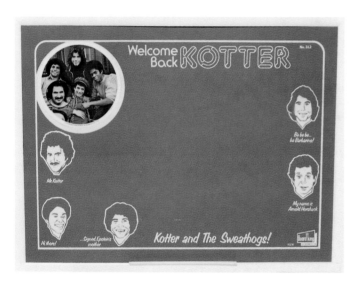

CHALKBOARD, Board King, 1976. $35.00 – $45.00.

COLORFORMS, Col-
orforms, 1976.
$10.00 – $15.00.

Left: COLORING BOOK #1081, Whitman, 1977. $8.00 – $10.00.

Right: COMIC BOOK, D.C., 1978.
Large 10" x 13" size. $5.00 – $8.00.

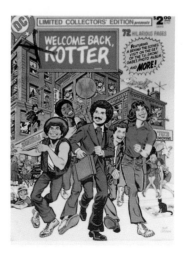

COMIC BOOKS, #1 – 10, D.C., 1977 – 1978. $3.00 – $5.00 each.

CUP, MUG, AND TUMBLER, Dawn, 1976. Mug not pictured.
$8.00 – $12.00 each.

DOLLS, Epstein, Washington, Horshack, Kotter, and Barbarino,
Mattel, 1976. $20.00 – $25.00 each.

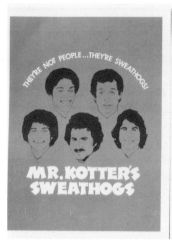

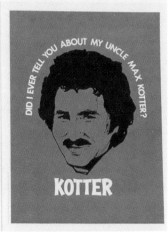

FOLDERS, Mead, 1977.
$3.00 – $5.00 each.

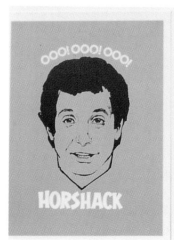

FRAME TRAY PUZZLES, Kotter and Cast, Whitman, 1977.
$8.00 – $10.00 each.

GOLDEN ALL-STAR BOOKS, Golden Press, 1977. Three different. #6413 and 6418 pictured. $5.00 – $8.00 each.

JIGSAW PUZZLES, HG Toys, 1976. Several different styles, #450-02 and #450-03 pictured. $8.00 – $12.00 each.

HALLOWEEN COSTUME, Kotter, Collegeville, 1976.
$15.00 – $20.00.

LUNCH BOX, Aladdin, 1977. Metal box with plastic thermos.
$25.00 – $30.00 box. $8.00 – $12.00 thermos.

MAGIC SLATES, Whitman, 1977. Two different styles.
$10.00 – $15.00 each.

NECKLACES, Wolper, 1978. Different styles including group illustration not pictured. $8.00 – $12.00 each.

Left: PAPERBACK BOOK, *The Sweathog Trail*, Ace Books, 1976. First printing of paperback #1 with different cover. $5.00 – $8.00.

Right: PAPERBACK BOOKS, #1 – 6, Tempo Books, 1976 – 1977. $3.00 – $5.00 each.

TRADING CARDS, Topps, 1976. 53 cards in set. Backs are made up of 8 puzzle cards and 45 Sweathogs' Speak cards.
$20.00 – $25.00 set. $.25 – $.50 single cards.
$2.00 – $3.00 wrapper. $10.00 – $15.00 display box.

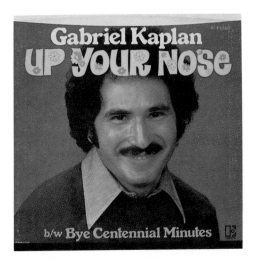

RECORD/LP, "Holes and Mello-Rolls," ABC Records, 1975. Comedy by Gabriel Kaplan. $8.00 – $10.00.

RECORD/45, "Up Your Nose"/"Bye Centennial Minutes," Elektra Records, 1976. Vocals by Gabriel Kaplan. $5.00 – $8.00.

RECORD CASES, Peerless Vid-Tronic Corp., 1976. Two sizes for LP's and 45's. Case for LP's pictured. $20.00 – $25.00 each.

VIEW-MASTER #J19, GAF, 1977. $10.00 – $15.00.

TV GUIDES, 1976 – 1978.
07/14/76 Kaplan and Strassman (not pictured); 01/01/77 Travolta; 10/22/77 Cast illustration; 11/04/78 Travolta illustrated. $3.00 – $5.00 each.

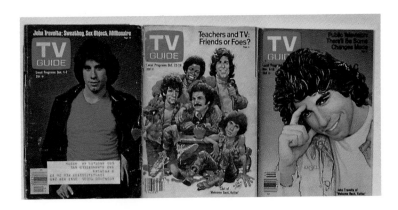

Other items not pictured:

WRISTWATCH, Barbarino, Pamco, 1976. Working watch with bright color display of Barbarino's face every few seconds. $35.00 – $45.00.

ACRYLIC PAINT BY NUMBER SETS, 1970s. Two styles. One with illustration of Kotter and Washington and the other with Kotter only. $20.00 – $25.00 each.

BEACH TOWEL, Barbarino, Wolper, 1976. Illustration of life-size Barbarino. $15.00 – $20.00.

BEANBAG CHAIR, Barbarino, 1970s. Large yellow chair with photo of Barbarino. $50.00 – $60.00.

BOARD GAME, Milton Bradley, 1977. $10.00 – $15.00.

BOOKCOVER, Barbarino, 1976. $8.00 – $10.00.

BRAIN TWISTER, Fleetwood, 1979. $10.00 – $15.00.

BULLETIN BOARD, 1970s. $35.00 – $45.00.

CANDY/TRADING CARDS, Phoenix, 1976. Eight cards in set. Cards came as a premium with boxed candy. $20.00 – $30.00 set; $3.00 – $4.00 single cards; $25.00 – $30.00 box.

DESK SET, Ahl Band, 1977. Four items, including figural stapler, pencil sharpener, memo pad, and calendar. $30.00 – $40.00.

GREETING CARDS, Metropolitan Greetings, 1970s. Set of 10 cards in box with cast photo on cover. $15.00 – $20.00.

HALLOWEEN COSTUME, Barbarino, Collegeville, 1976. $20.00 – $25.00.

JIGSAW PUZZLE, HG Toys, 1976. Giant 250 pieces. $15.00 – $20.00.

MECHANICAL ACTION BANK, Fleetwood, 1975. Grab-action bank of Horshack and Barbarino. $25.00 – $35.00.

MODEL KIT, Sweathogs Dream Machine, MPC, 1976. $25.00 – $35.00.

PAINT BY NUMBER SET, Sweathogs, Craft Master, 1976. $25.00 – $30.00.

PATCHES, 1970s. Different styles with illustrations of each character. $8.00 – $12.00 each.

PINBACK BUTTONS, 1970s. Several different styles for each character. $5.00 – $8.00 each.

PLAYSET, Toy Factory, 1976. Includes cardboard punch-outs of Kotter's classroom and cast members. $30.00 – $40.00.

POSTER ART KIT, 1970s. $20.00 – $25.00.

RECORD PLAYER, Peerless Vid-Tronic Corp., 1976. Cast photo. $35.00 – $45.00.

RECORD/45, "Welcome Back Kotter"/"Warm Baby," Reprise, 1976. Theme from the television show. Vocals by John Sebastian. Without picture sleeve. $3.00 – $5.00.

RINGS, 1970s. Metal rings of each character. $10.00 – $15.00 each.

SLEEPING BAG, 1970s. Illustration of cast on bag. $25.00 – $30.00.

SLIDE PUZZLE, 1976. Illustration of cast on card. $10.00 – $15.00.

SWEATHOGS GREASE MACHINE CARS, Ahi Brand, 1977. 5 different toy cars with figures. Each sold separately. $15.00 – $20.00 each.

TALKING VIEW-MASTER #TJ19. GAF, 1977. $20.00 – $25.00.

WASHINGTON SKATEBOARD FIGURE, Gabriel, 1977. Bendable character on card. $15.00 – $20.00.

WONDER WOMAN

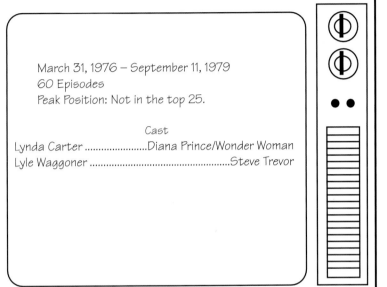

March 31, 1976 – September 11, 1979
60 Episodes
Peak Position: Not in the top 25.

Cast
Lynda Carter ....Diana Prince/Wonder Woman
Lyle Waggoner ....Steve Trevor

DOLLS, Wonder Woman, Diana Prince, Steve Trevor, Queen Hippolyte, Nubia, Mego, 1978. Wonder Woman and Steve Trevor pictured. $40.00 – $60.00 each.

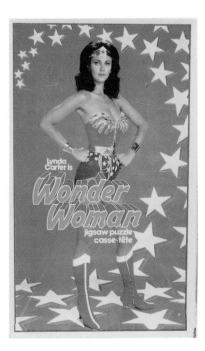

JIGSAW PUZZLE, APC, 1977.
$10.00 – $15.00.

JIGSAW PUZZLE, APC, 1978. $10.00 – $15.00.

RECORD/LP, "Portrait." Epic, 1978. Vocals by Lynda Carter.
$10.00 – $15.00.

RECORD/45, "Wonder Woman," Shadybrook Records, 1977.
Theme from the television show. Promotional copy with dupli-
cate B side. Vocals by the New World Symphony.
$10.00 – $15.00.

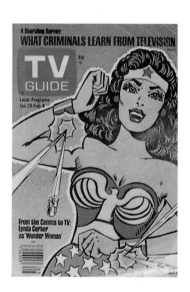

TV Guide.
01/29/77.
Lynda Carter as Wonder Woman.
$5.00 – $8.00.

Other items not pictured:

IRON-ONS, Lynda Carter, 1970s. Several different. $8.00 – $10.00 each.

JIGSAW PUZZLE, APC, 1978. Giant 27" x 43" size. $15.00 – $20.00.

JIGSAW PUZZLE, APC, 1970s. Photo cover of Lynda Carter in cape with blue background. $10.00 – $15.00.

JIGSAW PUZZLE, APC, 1970s. Illustrated cover with small photo of Lynda Carter in center. $8.00 – $12.00.

PLAYSET, Mego, 1978. For 12" dolls. $75.00 – $100.00.

POSTERS, 1970s. Various of Lynda Carter and Wonder Woman. $15.00 – $20.00 each.

RECORD/LP, "Portrait," Epic, 1978. Vocals by Lynda Carter. Picture disc version. $30.00 – $40.00.

RECORDS/45's Epic, 1978. "Toto"/"Put on a Show"; "All Night Song"/"Put on a Show." Vocals by Lynda Carter. Without picture sleeves. $5.00 – $8.00 each.

T-SHIRTS, 1970s. Various of Lynda Carter and Wonder Woman. $10.00 – $15.00 each.

TELEVISION'S HIT LIST

According to the A. C. Nielson's Top 25 Ratings
(listed by peak seasons)

#1	The Beverly Hillbillies	1962 – 1964
	Happy Days	1976 – 1977
	Laverne and Shirley	1977 – 1979
#2	Bewitched	1964 – 1965
	Three's Company	1978 – 1979
#3	Mork and Mindy	1978 – 1979

#4	Family Affair	1967 – 1968
	Charlie's Angels	1977 – 1978
#5	The Bionic Woman	1975 – 1976
	The Love Boat	1980 – 1981
#6	Green Acres	1966 – 1967
#7	Julia	1968 – 1969
	Good Times	1974 – 1975
	Little House on the Prairie	1977 – 1978
#8	The Waltons	1974 – 1975
#9	The Six Million Dollar Man	1975 – 1977

#11	Eight Is Enough	1978 – 1979
#13	Welcome Back Kotter	1976 – 1977
#16	The Partridge Family	1971 – 1972
	Starsky and Hutch	1975 – 1976
#17	Fantasy Island	1980 – 1981
#18	The Patty Duke Show	1963 – 1964
	Gilligan's Island	1964 – 1965
	CHiPs	1979 – 1980
#21	The Mod Squad	1971 – 1972
#25	Flipper	1964 – 1965

NOT IN THE TOP TWENTY-FIVE

The Brady Bunch
Donny and Marie
Family
The Flying Nun
Gidget
The Hardy Boys Mysteries
I Dream of Jeannie
Kung Fu
The Life and Times of Grizzly Adams
Nanny and the Professor
That Girl
Wonder Woman

SATURDAY MORNING SHOWS

(not rated)

The Brady Kids
The Bugaloos
Fonz and the Happy Days Gang
H. R. Pufnstuf
Jeannie
Josie and the Pussycats
The Krofft Supershow
Land of the Lost
Lidsville
The New Adventures of Gilligan
The New Zoo Revue
Sigmund and the Sea Monsters

BIBLIOGRAPHY

PERIODICALS

Card Collector's Price Guide. Plainview, New York: Century Publishing, 1995.

Spin Again Magazine. Los Angeles, California: Pilucho Press, 1993.

Tiger Beat Magazine. Hollywood, California: Laufer Publishing, 1975 – 1979.

Toy Shop. Iola, Wisconsin: Krause Publications, 1990 – 1995.

Toy Trader. Dubuque, Iowa: Antique Trader Publications, 1994 – 1995.

The Wrapper. St. Charles, Illinois: Les Davis. 1992 – 1995.

BOOKS

Aikins, Larry. *Pictorial Price Guide to Metal Lunch Boxes and Thermoses.* Gas City, Indiana: L-W Book Sales, 1992.

Benjamin, Christopher. *The Sport Americana Price Guide to the Non-Sports Cards.* Cleveland, Ohio: Edgewater Book Company, 1992.

Bruegman, Bill. *Toys of the Sixties.* Akron, Ohio: Cap'n Penny Productions, 1992.

Cox, Stephen. *The Beverly Hillbillies.* New York, New York: Harper Perennial Publishers, 1993.

Hake, Ted. *Hake's Guide to TV Collectibles.* Radnor, Pennsylvania: Wallace-Homestead, 1990.

Lofman, Ron. *Goldmine's Celebrity Vocals.* Iola, Wisconsin: Krause Publications, 1994.

Monsuh, Barry. *International Television and Video Almanac.* New York, New York: Quigley Publishing Co., 1995.

Overstreet, Robert M. *The Overstreet Comic Book Price Guide.* New York, New York: Avon Books, 1995.

Terrace, Vincent. *Encyclopedia of Television Series, Pilots and Specials.* New York: New York: Baseline Publishing, 1985.

Young, Mary. *Tomart's Price Guide to Lowe & Whitman Paper Dolls.* Dayton, Ohio: Tomart Publishing, 1993.

Ziller, Dian. *Collectible Coloring Books.* West Chester, Pennsylvania: Schiffer Publishing, 1992.

INDEX

TV Memorabilia

COLLECTOR BOOKS

Informing Today's Collector

For over two decades we have been keeping collectors informed on trends and values in all fields of antiques and collectibles.

DOLLS, FIGURES & TEDDY BEARS

2382	**Advertising Dolls**, Identification & Values, Robison & Sellers	$9.95
2079	**Barbie** Doll Fashions, Volume I, Eames	$24.95
3957	**Barbie** Exclusives, Rana	$18.95
4557	**Barbie**, The First 30 Years, Deutsch	$24.95
3310	**Black Dolls**, 1820–1991, Perkins	$17.95
3873	**Black Dolls**, Book II, Perkins	$17.95
3810	**Chatty Cathy** Dolls, Lewis	$15.95
2021	Collectible **Action Figures**, 2nd Ed., Manos	$14.95
1529	Collector's Encyclopedia of **Barbie** Dolls, DeWein	$19.95
4506	Collector's Guide to **Dolls in Uniform**, Bourgeois	$18.95
3727	Collector's Guide to **Ideal Dolls**, Izen	$18.95
3728	Collector's Guide to Miniature **Teddy Bears**, Powell	$17.95
3967	Collector's Guide to **Trolls**, Peterson	$19.95
4569	**Howdy Doody**, Collector's Reference and Trivia Guide, Koch	$16.95
1067	**Madame Alexander** Dolls, Smith	$19.95
3971	**Madame Alexander** Dolls Price Guide #20, Smith	$9.95
3733	**Modern Collector's** Dolls, Sixth Series, Smith	$24.95
3991	**Modern Collector's** Dolls, Seventh Series, Smith	$24.95
4571	**Liddle Kiddles**, Identification & Value Guide, Langford	$18.95
3972	Patricia Smith's **Doll Values**, Antique to Modern, 11th Edition	$12.95
3826	Story of **Barbie**, Westenhouser	$19.95
1513	**Teddy Bears & Steiff** Animals, Mandel	$9.95
1817	**Teddy Bears & Steiff** Animals, 2nd Series, Mandel	$19.95
2084	**Teddy Bears, Annalee's & Steiff** Animals, 3rd Series, Mandel	$19.95
1808	Wonder of **Barbie**, Manos	$9.95
1430	World of **Barbie** Dolls, Manos	$9.95

FURNITURE

1457	American **Oak** Furniture, McNerney	$9.95
3716	American **Oak** Furniture, Book II, McNerney	$12.95
1118	Antique **Oak** Furniture, Hill	$7.95
2132	Collector's Encyclopedia of **American** Furniture, Vol. I, Swedberg	$24.95
2271	Collector's Encyclopedia of **American** Furniture, Vol. II, Swedberg	$24.95
3720	Collector's Encyclopedia of **American** Furniture, Vol. III, Swedberg	$24.95
1437	Collector's Guide to **Country** Furniture, Raycraft	$9.95
3878	Collector's Guide to **Oak** Furniture, George	$12.95
1755	Furniture of the **Depression Era**, Swedberg	$19.95
3906	**Heywood-Wakefield** Modern Furniture, Rouland	$18.95
1965	**Pine** Furniture, Our American Heritage, McNerney	$14.95
1885	**Victorian** Furniture, Our American Heritage, McNerney	$9.95
3829	**Victorian** Furniture, Our American Heritage, Book II, McNerney	$9.95
3869	**Victorian** Furniture books, 2 volume set, McNerney	$19.90

JEWELRY, HATPINS, WATCHES & PURSES

1712	Antique & Collector's **Thimbles** & Accessories, Mathis	$19.95
1748	Antique **Purses**, Revised Second Ed., Holiner	$19.95
1278	Art Nouveau & Art Deco **Jewelry**, Baker	$9.95
4558	**Christmas Pins**, Past and Present, Gallina	$18.95
3875	Collecting Antique **Stickpins**, Kerins	$16.95
3722	Collector's Ency. of **Compacts, Carryalls & Face Powder Boxes**, Mueller	$24.95
3992	Complete Price Guide to **Watches**, #15, Shugart	$21.95
1716	Fifty Years of Collectible **Fashion Jewelry**, 1925-1975, Baker	$19.95
1424	**Hatpins** & Hatpin Holders, Baker	$9.95
4570	Ladies' **Compacts**, Gerson	$24.95
1181	100 Years of Collectible **Jewelry**, 1850-1950, Baker	$9.95
2348	20th Century Fashionable Plastic **Jewelry**, Baker	$19.95
3830	Vintage **Vanity Bags & Purses**, Gerson	$24.95

TOYS, MARBLES & CHRISTMAS COLLECTIBLES

3427	**Advertising Character** Collectibles, Dotz	$17.95
2333	Antique & Collector's **Marbles**, 3rd Ed., Grist	$9.95
3827	Antique & Collector's **Toys**, 1870–1950, Longest	$24.95
3956	Baby Boomer **Games**, Identification & Value Guide, Polizzi	$24.95
3717	**Christmas** Collectibles, 2nd Edition, Whitmyer	$24.95
1752	**Christmas** Ornaments, Lights & Decorations, Johnson	$19.95
3874	Collectible Coca-Cola Toy **Trucks**, deCourtivron	$24.95
2338	Collector's Encyclopedia of **Disneyana**, Longest, Stern	$24.95
2151	Collector's Guide to **Tootsietoys**, 2nd Ed., Richter	$16.95
3436	Grist's Big Book of **Marbles**	$19.95
3970	Grist's Machine-Made & Contemporary **Marbles**, 2nd Ed.	$9.95
3732	**Matchbox®** Toys, 1948 to 1993, Johnson	$18.95
3823	**Mego** Toys, An Illustrated Value Guide, Chrouch	15.95
1540	**Modern Toys** 1930–1980, Baker	$19.95
3888	**Motorcycle** Toys, Antique & Contemporary, Gentry/Downs	$18.95
3891	Schroeder's Collectible **Toys**, Antique to Modern Price Guide, 2nd Ed.	$17.95
1886	Stern's Guide to **Disney** Collectibles	$14.95
2139	Stern's Guide to **Disney** Collectibles, 2nd Series	$14.95
3975	Stern's Guide to **Disney** Collectibles, 3rd Series	$18.95
2028	**Toys**, Antique & Collectible, Longest	$14.95
3975	**Zany Characters** of the Ad World, Lamphier	$16.95

INDIANS, GUNS, KNIVES, TOOLS, PRIMITIVES

1868	Antique **Tools**, Our American Heritage, McNerney	$9.95
2015	Archaic **Indian** Points & Knives, Edler	$14.95
1426	**Arrowheads** & Projectile Points, Hothem	$7.95
2279	**Indian** Artifacts of the Midwest, Hothem	$14.95
3885	**Indian** Artifacts of the Midwest, Book II, Hothem	$16.95
1964	**Indian** Axes & Related Stone Artifacts, Hothem	$14.95
2023	**Keen Kutter** Collectibles, Heuring	$14.95
3887	Modern **Guns**, Identification & Values, 10th Ed., Quertermous	$12.95
4505	Standard Guide to **Razors**, Ritchie & Stewart	$9.95
3325	Standard **Knife** Collector's Guide, 2nd Ed., Ritchie & Stewart	$12.95

PAPER COLLECTIBLES & BOOKS

1441	Collector's Guide to **Post Cards**, Wood	$9.95
2081	Guide to Collecting **Cookbooks**, Allen	$14.95
3969	Huxford's **Old Book** Value Guide, 7th Ed.	$19.95
3821	Huxford's **Paperback** Value Guide	$19.95
2080	Price Guide to **Cookbooks & Recipe Leaflets**, Dickinson	$9.95
2346	**Sheet Music** Reference & Price Guide, 2nd Ed., Pafik & Guiheen	$18.95

GLASSWARE

1006	**Cambridge Glass** Reprint 1930–1934	$14.95
1007	**Cambridge Glass** Reprint 1949–1953	$14.95
2310	**Children's Glass Dishes**, China & Furniture, Vol. I, Lechler	$19.95
1627	**Children's Glass Dishes**, China & Furniture, Vol. II, Lechler	$19.95
4561	Collectible **Drinking Glasses**, Chase & Kelly	$17.95
3719	Coll. **Glassware** from the 40's, 50's & 60's, 3rd Ed., Florence	$19.95
2352	Collector's Encyclopedia of **Akro Agate Glassware**, Florence	$14.95
1810	Collector's Encyclopedia of **American Art Glass**, Shuman	$29.95
3312	Collector's Encyclopedia of **Children's Dishes**, Whitmyer	$19.95
3724	Collector's Encyclopedia of **Depression Glass**, 12th Ed., Florence	$19.95
1664	Collector's Encyclopedia of **Heisey Glass**, 1925–1938, Bredehoft	$24.95
3905	Collector's Encyclopedia of **Milk Glass**, Newbound	$24.95
1523	Colors In **Cambridge Glass**, National Cambridge Soceity	$19.95

COLLECTOR BOOKS
Informing Today's Collector

4564	**Crackle Glass**, Weitman	$18.95
2275	**Czechoslovakian Glass** and Collectibles, Barta	$16.95
3882	**Elegant Glassware** of the Depression Era, 6th Ed., Florence	$19.95
1380	Encylopedia of **Pattern Glass**, McClain	$12.95
3981	Ever's Standard **Cut Glass** Value Guide	$12.95
3725	**Fostoria**, Pressed, Blown & Hand Molded Shapes, Kerr	$24.95
3883	**Fostoria Stemware**, The Crystal for America, Long & Seate	$24.95
3318	**Glass Animals** of the Depression Era, Garmon & Spencer	$19.95
3886	**Kitchen Glassware** of the Depression Years, 5th Ed., Florence	$19.95
2394	**Oil Lamps II**, Glass Kerosene Lamps, Thuro	$24.95
3889	Pocket Guide to **Depression Glass**, 9th Ed., Florence	$9.95
3739	Standard Encylopedia of **Carnival Glass**, 4th Ed., Edwards	$24.95
3740	Standard **Carnival Glass** Price Guide, 9th Ed.	$9.95
3974	Standard Encylopedia of **Opalescent Glass**, Edwards	$19.95
1848	**Very Rare Glassware** of the Depression Years, Florence	$24.95
2140	**Very Rare Glassware** of the Depression Years, 2nd Series, Florence	$24.95
3326	**Very Rare Glassware** of the Depression Years, 3rd Series, Florence	$24.95
3909	**Very Rare Glassware** of the Depression Years, 4th Series, Florence	$24.95
2224	World of **Salt Shakers**, 2nd Ed., Lechner	$24.95

POTTERY

1312	**Blue & White Stoneware**, McNerney	$9.95
1958	So. Potteries **Blue Ridge Dinnerware**, 3rd Ed., Newbound	$14.95
1959	**Blue Willow**, 2nd Ed., Gaston	$14.95
3816	Collectible **Vernon Kilns**, Nelson	$24.95
3311	Collecting **Yellow Ware** – Id. & Value Guide, McAllister	$16.95
1373	Collector's Encyclopedia of **American Dinnerware**, Cunningham	$24.95
3815	Collector's Encyclopedia of **Blue Ridge Dinnerware**, Newbound	$19.95
2272	Collector's Encyclopedia of **California Pottery**, Chipman	$24.95
3811	Collector's Encyclopedia of **Colorado Pottery**, Carlton	$24.95
2133	Collector's Encyclopedia of **Cookie Jars**, Roerig	$24.95
3723	Collector's Encyclopedia of **Cookie Jars**, Volume II, Roerig	$24.95
3429	Collector's Encyclopedia of **Cowan Pottery**, Saloff	$24.95
2209	Collector's Encyclopedia of **Fiesta**, 7th Ed., Huxford	$19.95
3961	Collector's Encyclopedia of **Early Noritake**, Alden	$24.95
1439	Collector's Encyclopedia of **Flow Blue China**, Gaston	$19.95
3812	Collector's Encyclopedia of **Flow Blue China**, 2nd Ed., Gaston	$24.95
3813	Collector's Encyclopedia of **Hall China**, 2nd Ed., Whitmyer	$24.95
3431	Collector's Encyclopedia of **Homer Laughlin China**, Jasper	$24.95
1276	Collector's Encyclopedia of **Hull Pottery**, Roberts	$19.95
4573	Collector's Encyclopedia of **Knowles, Taylor & Knowles**, Gaston	$24.95
3962	Collector's Encyclopedia of **Lefton China**, DeLozier	$19.95
2210	Collector's Encyclopedia of **Limoges Porcelain**, 2nd Ed., Gaston	$24.95
2334	Collector's Encyclopedia of **Majolica Pottery**, Katz-Marks	$19.95
1358	Collector's Encyclopedia of **McCoy Pottery**, Huxford	$19.95
3963	Collector's Encyclopedia of **Metlox Potteries**, Gibbs Jr.	$24.95
3313	Collector's Encyclopedia of **Niloak**, Gifford	$19.95
3837	Collector's Encyclopedia of **Nippon Porcelain I**, Van Patten	$24.95
2089	Collector's Ency. of **Nippon Porcelain**, 2nd Series, Van Patten	$24.95
1665	Collector's Ency. of **Nippon Porcelain**, 3rd Series, Van Patten	$24.95
3836	**Nippon Porcelain** Price Guide, Van Patten	$9.95
1447	Collector's Encyclopedia of **Noritake**, Van Patten	$19.95
3432	Collector's Encyclopedia of **Noritake**, 2nd Series, Van Patten	$24.95
1037	Collector's Encyclopedia of **Occupied Japan**, Vol. I, Florence	$14.95
1038	Collector's Encyclopedia of **Occupied Japan**, Vol. II, Florence	$14.95
2088	Collector's Encyclopedia of **Occupied Japan**, Vol. III, Florence	$14.95
2019	Collector's Encyclopedia of **Occupied Japan**, Vol. IV, Florence	$14.95
2335	Collector's Encyclopedia of **Occupied Japan**, Vol. V, Florence	$14.95
3964	Collector's Encyclopedia of **Pickard China**, Reed	$24.95
1311	Collector's Encyclopedia of **R.S. Prussia**, 1st Series, Gaston	$24.95
1715	Collector's Encyclopedia of **R.S. Prussia**, 2nd Series, Gaston	$24.95
3726	Collector's Encyclopedia of **R.S. Prussia**, 3rd Series, Gaston	$24.95
3877	Collector's Encyclopedia of **R.S. Prussia**, 4th Series, Gaston	$24.95
1034	Collector's Encyclopedia of **Roseville Pottery**, Huxford	$19.95
1035	Collector's Encyclopedia of **Roseville Pottery**, 2nd Ed., Huxford	$19.95
3357	**Roseville** Price Guide No. 10	$9.95
2083	Collector's Encyclopedia of **Russel Wright** Designs, Kerr	$19.95
3965	Collector's Encyclopedia of **Sascha Brastoff**, Conti, Bethany & Seay	$24.95

3314	Collector's Encyclopedia of **Van Briggle** Art Pottery, Sasicki	$24.95
2111	Collector's Encyclopedia of **Weller Pottery**, Huxford	$29.95
3452	Coll. Guide to Country Stoneware & Pottery, Raycraft	$11.95
2077	Coll. Guide to **Country Stoneware & Pottery**, 2nd Series, Raycraft	$14.95
3433	Collector's Guide To **Harker Pottery** - U.S.A., Colbert	$17.95
3434	Coll. Guide to **Hull Pottery**, The Dinnerware Line, Gick-Burke	$16.95
3876	Collector's Guide to **Lu-Ray Pastels**, Meehan	$18.95
3814	Collector's Guide to **Made in Japan** Ceramics, White	$18.95
4565	Collector's Guide to **Rockingham**, The Enduring Ware, Brewer	$14.95
2339	Collector's Guide to **Shawnee Pottery**, Vanderbilt	$19.95
1425	**Cookie Jars**, Westfall	$9.95
3440	**Cookie Jars**, Book II, Westfall	$19.95
3435	Debolt's Dictionary of **American Pottery Marks**	$17.95
2379	Lehner's Ency. of **U.S. Marks** on Pottery, Porcelain & China	$24.95
3825	**Puritan Pottery**, Morris	$24.95
1670	**Red Wing Collectibles**, DePasquale	$9.95
1440	**Red Wing Stoneware**, DePasquale	$9.95
3738	**Shawnee Pottery**, Mangus	$24.95
3327	**Watt Pottery** – Identification & Value Guide, Morris	$19.95

OTHER COLLECTIBLES

2269	Antique **Brass & Copper** Collectibles, Gaston	$16.95
1880	Antique **Iron**, McNerney	$9.95
3872	Antique **Tins**, Dodge	$24.95
1714	**Black** Collectibles, Gibbs	$19.95
1128	**Bottle** Pricing Guide, 3rd Ed., Cleveland	$7.95
3959	**Cereal Box** Bonanza, The 1950's, Bruce	$19.95
3718	Collectible **Aluminum**, Grist	$16.95
3445	Collectible **Cats**, An Identification & Value Guide, Fyke	$18.95
4560	Collectible **Cats**, An Identification & Value Guide, Book II, Fyke	$19.95
4563	Collector's Encyclopedia of **Wall Pockets**, Newbound	$19.95
1634	Collector's Ency. of Figural & Novelty **Salt & Pepper Shakers**, Davern	$19.95
2020	Collector's Ency. of Figural & Novelty **Salt & Pepper Shakers**, Vol. II, Davern	$19.95
2018	Collector's Encyclopedia of **Granite Ware**, Greguire	$24.95
3430	Collector's Encyclopedia of **Granite Ware**, Book II, Greguire	$24.95
3879	Collector's Guide to **Antique Radios**, 3rd Ed., Bunis	$18.95
1916	Collector's Guide to **Art Deco**, Gaston	$14.95
3880	Collector's Guide to **Cigarette Lighters**, Flanagan	$17.95
1537	Collector's Guide to **Country Baskets**, Raycraft	$9.95
3966	Collector's Guide to **Inkwells**, Identification & Values, Badders	$18.95
3881	Collector's Guide to **Novelty Radios**, Bunis/Breed	$18.95
3729	Collector's Guide to **Snow Domes**, Guarnaccia	$18.95
3730	Collector's Guide to **Transistor Radios**, Bunis	$15.95
2276	**Decoys**, Kangas	$24.95
1629	**Doorstops**, Identification & Values, Bertoia	$9.95
4567	Figural **Napkin Rings**, Gottschalk & Whitson	$18.95
3968	**Fishing Lure** Collectibles, Murphy/Edmisten	$24.95
3817	**Flea Market Trader**, 10th Ed., Huxford	$12.95
3976	Foremost Guide to **Uncle Sam** Collectibles, Czulewicz	$24.95
3819	**General Store Collectibles**, Wilson	$24.95
2215	Goldstein's **Coca-Cola** Collectibles	$16.95
3884	Huxford's Collectible **Advertising**, 2nd Ed.	$24.95
2216	**Kitchen Antiques**, 1790–1940, McNerney	$14.95
3321	Ornamental & Figural **Nutcrackers**, Rittenhouse	$16.95
2026	**Railroad** Collectibles, 4th Ed., Baker	$14.95
1632	**Salt & Pepper Shakers**, Guarnaccia	$9.95
1888	**Salt & Pepper Shakers** II, Identification & Value Guide, Book II, Guarnaccia	$14.95
2220	**Salt & Pepper Shakers** III, Guarnaccia	$14.95
3443	**Salt & Pepper Shakers** IV, Guarnaccia	$18.95
4555	**Schroeder's Antiques** Price Guide, 14th Ed., Huxford	$14.95
2096	**Silverplated Flatware**, Revised 4th Edition, Hagan	$14.95
1922	Standard **Old Bottle** Price Guide, Sellari	$14.95
3892	**Toy & Miniature Sewing Machines**, Thomas	$18.95
3828	Value Guide to **Advertising Memorabilia**, Summers	$18.95
3977	Value Guide to **Gas Station** Memorabilia, Summers & Priddy	$24.95
4572	**Wall Pockets** of the Past, Perkins	$17.95
3444	**Wanted to Buy**, 5th Edition	$9.95